Powell's   Rameses: The Forgotten Star (NoDJ)

45.00/3.98   **NDJ**

Film, Television & Theater   97155

RAMESES
THE FORGOTTEN STAR

RAMESES
THE FORGOTTEN STAR
Chris Woodward

Rameses the Forgotten Star
By Chris Woodward
Edited by Noah Levine

Layout and design by Kevin McGroarty

Copyright © 2011 by Chris Woodward. All rights reserved. No part of this publication may be reproduced or transmitted in any form or by any means, now known or to be invented, without written permission from the publisher.

Squash Publishing
Chicago, IL 60640
www.squashpublishing.com

ISBN 10: 0-9744681-7-7
ISBN 13: 978-0-9744681-7-4

First Edition
6 5 4 3 2 1

DEDICATION

I dedicate this book to three of magic's giants: Jay Marshall, Patrick Page, and Charles Reynolds who all left us far too soon. And to another giant, Sir Tim Berners-Lee, for without the world-wide-web this book would never have been possible.

❦ FOREWORD

Edwin A. Dawes

FOR ANY STUDENT OF MAGIC'S colourful history the Edwardian period in Britain is an extremely fascinating one. The old image of the nineteenth-century music halls had by now been dispelled by the building of handsome new Variety theatres, which not only attracted packed houses twice nightly but simultaneously conferred respectability that ensured patronage by the middle classes who formerly would have shunned such venues. Against this background there was a positive avalanche of magicians bringing a wealth of different styles of performance, ranging across sleight of hand, escapology, comedy and grand scale illusions. This was the period that ushered in what I often refer to as the 'American Magical Invasion' of Britain, initiated in 1899 by T. Nelson Downs, the 'King of Koins,' and quickly followed in the first decade of the 20th century by compatriots Howard Thurston, Chung Ling Soo, Houdini, The Great Lafayette, Horace Goldin, Arnold De Biere and Imro Fox, performers whose names have endured in the annals of magic.

Of course, these stars were by no means the only magicians treading the British Variety boards. The period up to the outbreak of the First World War in 1914 can justly be hailed as a Golden Age for magic when one savours a galaxy of such richness as Servais Le Roy, Charles Morritt, Okito, Carl Hertz, Oswald Williams, Selbit,

Dr. Walford Bodie, Clement De Lion, Lewis Davenport and David Devant, not forgetting the lady performers Talma, Adelaide Herrmann and Vonetta, all of whom provided characteristic styles to enchant their audiences.

Impressive, too, is the contribution made to magic by Jewish performers and over thirty years ago I devoted a chapter in *The Great Illusionists* to what was termed 'The Jewish Connexion,' dating back to Jacob Philadelphia in the 18th century. It is illuminating that five of the seven magicians named above in the 'American invasion' were Jews. But two British Jewish performers were embarking on careers in the first decade of the twentieth century, the young Cecil Lyle and the subject of this book, Albert Marchinski, a Russian-Polish immigrant, who took his bow in 1908 in the guise of an Egyptian wonder worker, Rameses, presenting some remarkable illusions. At this time costume acts, such as Chung Ling Soo's Chinese theme, Fasola's characterisation and Linga Singh's authentic Indian performance, were very popular and Marchinski was a welcome addition to the genre. Not only that, but he was able to reverse the 'invasion' with two acclaimed tours of America as well as other overseas engagements.

Strangely, Marchinski has received relatively little attention in the standard texts on magic history and consequently the present biography by Chris Woodward is to be warmly welcomed. He has discovered there is considerable information about Marchinski scattered widely in the specialist literature and general press, which, thanks to modern technology, he has been able to access and assemble; this compilation, coupled with the fact that his late father-in-law Maurice Fogel actually worked for Marchinski toward the end of the illusionist's career, and taken together with the fruits of his assiduous research for family and friends, enables the reader to gain an insight to the illusionist's personal life with its worrying financial troubles, his spectacular magic, and the pleasure he brought to the thousands of theatre patrons around the world during his twenty-two years as Rameses. ✻

For the concert of life, no one has a programme......

PROLOGUE

❧LIGHTNING *CAN* STRIKE TWICE.

THE NEW EMPIRE THEATRE in the costal hamlet of Southend, Essex, was a variety hall that had faded from prominence like many others. But in contrast to many similar halls, the New Empire, by 2008, had been reopened and was turning a small profit, thanks to the devotion of a group of local enthusiasts that organized The New Empire Theatre Fund. Such was their commitment to the theatre that local fundraising activities were staged to keep the hall's old doors open.

The building's interior was redecorated, amateur theatricals were staged, and professional artists trod the boards, too. The New Empire's profile was on the rise.

Considering the improvements and efforts made on the theatre's behalf, a notice from the landlord telling the leaseholders to vacate – virtually without notice – came as something of a shock. They would have to vacate a property that they looked upon as a second home and had come to love. With no alternative or possible appeal they immediately started to pack up and remove everything belonging to them, only to receive a double blow when they were told that the fourteen days notice had been reduced to seven; and unless everything was removed by that date, the locks would be changed and they would lose everything. Props and costumes were hurriedly removed and brought to storage facilities scattered around Southend, in garages, private homes, stores and lock-ups. With just hours to go everything was removed. It was alleged that the tenants had been living a hand-to-mouth existence, raising funds to pay the rent. When they fell behind with those payments, the current owner – who had been waiting for the rent that never materialised – decided he'd had enough, and called it a day.

Was the building jinxed? Or was this a simple case of history repeating itself?

In the summer of 1917, some ninety years earlier, Albert "Rameses" Marchinski leased the New Empire Theatre in Southend. At enormous expense to the new tenant, the theatre was re-seated and redecorated, outfitted with new, plush fittings from top to bottom.

Perhaps ironically, upon the theatre's reopening, the first production staged by Marchinski was *Damaged Goods*. Will Goldston reported on it in *The Magician Monthly*:

> RAMESES, the Oriental [sic] magician, will in future be seen in a new role, and for a magician, an unusual one. He is opening the Empire, Southend-on-Sea, with the controversial and much discussed play, 'Damaged Goods', on Monday, August 6th.
>
> Many improvements have been effected in the house itself as to seating and convenience of ingress and egress, and all upholstering etc., has been entirely renewed. Mr. T. Graham Macdona will act as resident Manager, and an attractive programme of theatrical pieces has been decided upon. Rameses has our cordial good wishes for success in the capacity of theatrical proprietor.[1]

The following week, Marchinski, still the sole lessee of the theatre, presented twice nightly the charming military drama *The Prince and the Beggarmaid*. This was followed the next week by the screaming farcical comedy *The Glad Eye*.

The production changed on September 3rd to Marchinski's own show supplemented by a full London Vaudeville Company.

On April 8th 1918 a grand complimentary benefit was presented at The Empire Theatre with The Great Rameses supported by a full Star Company.

But less than twelve months later, things went wrong, and tragically so. For the week commencing June 24th 1918 "Albert Rameses" on behalf of Rameses Amusements Limited & Sydney Bransgrove presented as a "Special Attraction" London's biggest laugh *Ye Gods*. It was an apt title, for he had tried everything to keep the short-lived lease at the Empire a profitable one. Within a month, the following appeared in the local newspaper:

1918 July 4th Debtors
RAMESES AMUSEMENTS LIMITED - RAMESES' MISFORTUNES

At the offices of the official receiver for the Chelmsford district Bedford Row, (London) W.C., on Monday last, before, Mr. E. W. J. Savill, senior official receiver for the Southend and Chelmsford districts, this first meeting of creditors was held under the failure re Albert Rameses, lately carrying on business or residing at the Empire Theatre, Alexandra Street, Southend-on Sea, theatrical manager and artist, when it was decided to appoint Mr. Frederick Seymour Salaman, chartered accountant, of 1 Bucklersbury, E.C., as trustee of the estate to act in conjunction with a committee of inspection which was also appointed, the trustee's bond being fixed at £100.

The statement of affairs filed by the debtor disclosed gross liabilities amounting to £3,658 8s. 6d. of which £3,528 19s. 6d. was due to unsecured creditors. To preferential creditors, for rent, £81.10s., for rates, etc., £48, making the, total ranking liabilities amount to £3,658 8s. 6d.

The assets consisted of shares in Rameses Amusements, Ltd. (of no value), book debts £1,524.11s., returned as being valueless, thus, leaving a deficiency of £3,658 8s. 6d.

The debtor alleged his failure to have been caused through loss of money at the Empire Theatre, Southend-on-Sea, the failure of which was chiefly brought about by air-raids.'

He accounted for his deficiency as follows: Net loss arising from carrying on business from May 19, 1917, until April, 1918, £1,500; bad debts, £1,524. 11s.; household and personal expenses from May 19, 1917, £1,500; depreciation in shares in Rameses Amusements, Ltd., £2,000; shares in Rameses Amusements, Ltd., given to wife, £1,000; shares in Rameses Amusements, Ltd., given to A. Leigh, £500; interest to moneylenders, £350, making a total of £7,374 11s., less excess of assets over liabilities on May 19, 1917, £3,716 2s 6d., leaving a net deficiency of £3,658 8s. 6d. as shown in the statement of affairs.

Rameses excuse for the failure? "The 1914/1918 world war had taken its toll," or so he claimed.

His was a textbook case of rags to riches, then back again. He came from a humble but well-respected family, but plunged into the world of theatre and variety; as he trod the boards, his name and fortune were made. He topped bills, appeared before Royalty, and then tumbled back down from whence he'd come, appearing twice nightly.

The life of Albert Marchinski was one highlighted by aspirations and dreams that, once attained, could not be maintained. This is the story of one forgotten star's rise and fall – and rise again.

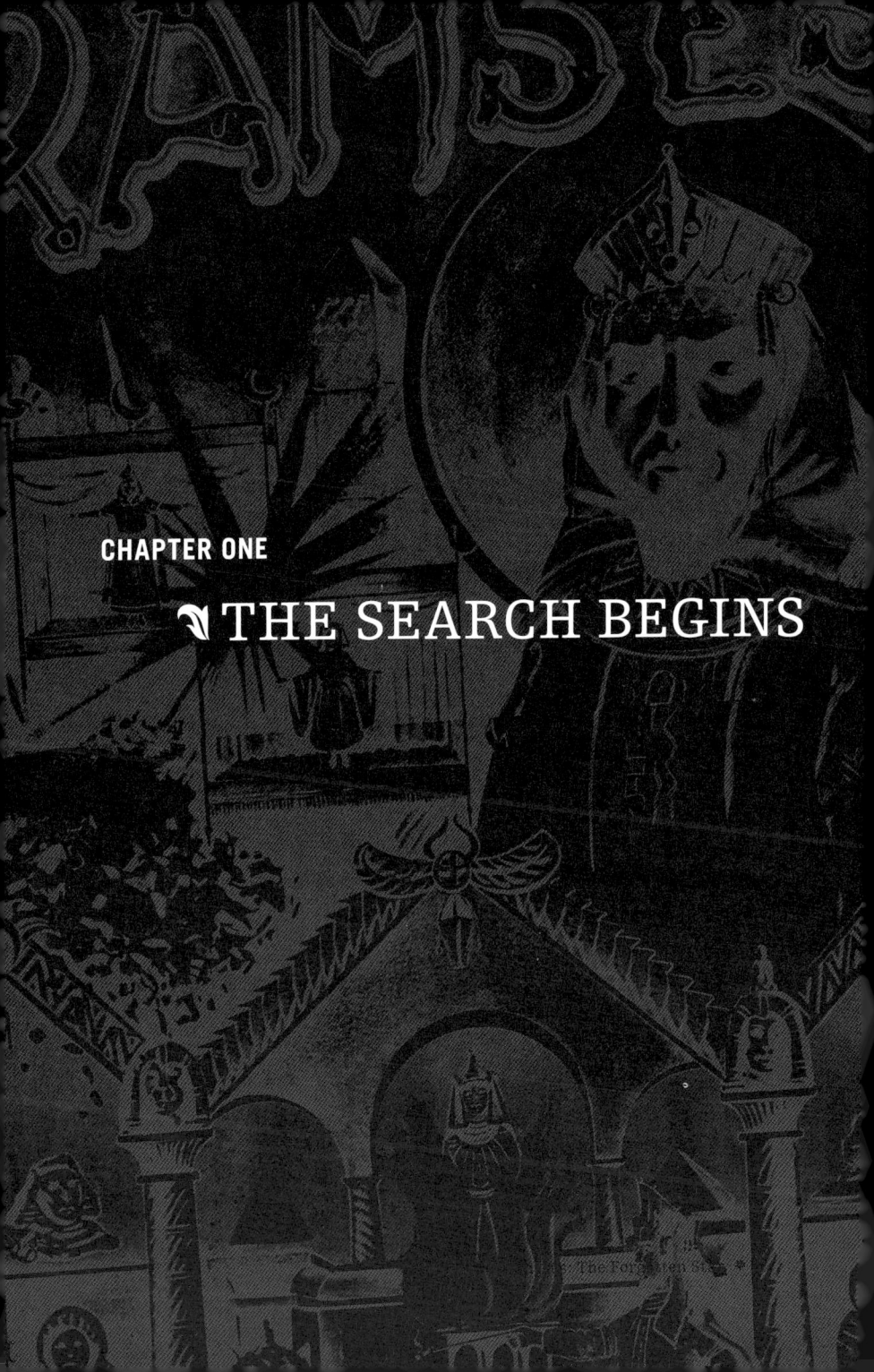

CHAPTER ONE

THE SEARCH BEGINS

IN 1975 PATRICK PAGE first alerted me to the wonderful pictorial reference book *100 Years of Magic Posters* by Charles and Regina Reynolds. As I was eager to obtain a copy of this book, my father-in-law Maurice Fogel found a pristine autographed copy for me while working in New York. It is a book that I still cherish, as do I the long established friendship of Regina and the late Charles Reynolds. Within this book is a reference to *Rameses the Royal Illusionist,* whose real name was Albert Marchinski. When this poster book was being researched in the early 1970's, Maurice told Charles and Regina that his mother was a relative of Rameses. It wasn't a case of "their cat jumped over our wall, so we are related" they really *were* on the same family tree.

Albert Marchinski, (sometimes spelled "Marchinsky") who appeared as *Rameses, The Egyptian Wonder Worker*, was born in Poland in 1876. Shortly afterwards, his parents Philip and Eva, who were born in Kovno, escaped the pogroms by moving the family to London. They lived at 9 St. Peter's Road, Mile End, in the east end. By 1895 they were living on 114 Spelman Street. Philip and Eva were highly respected members of the Jewish community, so much so that when they died, they were buried in Grave A Row #1 at the Edmonton Cemetery in east London.

His father Philip was a highly respected military clothing manufacturer with connections extending as far as South Africa. Albert had three brothers: Lesser who was born in 1883, Abe who was born two years later, (both would become Albert's assistants), and Izzy, who was born 1891. There were also five sisters: Lily, Sara, Rachel, Katie and Pearl. Eva and Philip had many mouths to feed!

Young Albert was first inspired by magic, at 14, while watching a magician perform at the old Aquarium in London. In 1890 he started performing a full show at small halls in and around London. During this period Tom Barrasford allowed Marchinski to rehearse his new illusion show for free for six weeks at the Britannia Theatre. He received encouragement from the magic dealer Joseph Bland of 35 New Oxford St., from whom he bought his first apparatus and through whom he received many engagements.

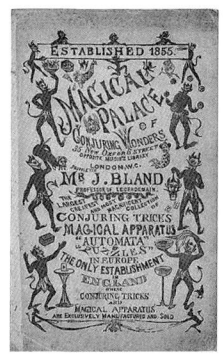

Albert was a diligent student of the mystic art and was not satisfied with travelling the beaten path. Instead, he marked out a route of his own, not by inventing new tricks, but by presenting the old and well tried in a new and original guise. He evolved an act which for "weird beauty, brilliancy and effectiveness of design, stage setting and rapidity of action had no parallel in vaudeville magic."[1] As he was aware of the potential competition at that time, and with William Robinson playing the Chinese character Chung Ling Soo, and Linga Singh appearing in Indian dress, he decided to take on the role of the famous Egyptian Pharaoh Rameses.

In his wonderful book *P.T. Selbit Magical Innovator,* Peter Warlock explains how Marchinski changed the spelling of his stage name from "Ramasis" to "Ramases," and finally to "Rameses" in order

The Search Begins ✹ 9

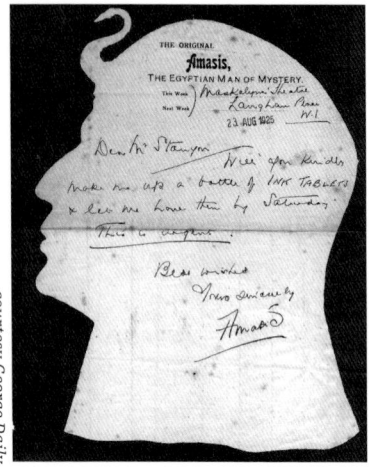

courtesy George Daily

to distance himself from the other Egyptian dressed performer "Amasis."

One profound influence on Marchinski's life was "Professor" Harcourt. Harcourt had caused a sensation in 1901 at the Hull Empire theatre with his "flying lady illusion." A former Vice President of *The Magic Circle* James Esler wrote in one of his notebooks:

> You may search the world over and you won't find another conjurer exactly like Fred Harcourt. It is possible that you might find a better one but I have my doubts. You will certainly not find a more entertaining or gentlemanly one.

Fred Harcourt died in January of 1906 at the early age of 39. Shortly afterwards, Albert made a decision that would greatly change the course of his life. He acquired all of Harcourt's props and illusions from his widow Lillian. The item that most caught his artistic eye was the levitation Lilith.

Sadly, little has been written about Rameses. I find this surprising, since he certainly gained success as a spectacular "bill topper." It is particularly surprising that Rameses is not mentioned in Holden's *Programmes of Famous Magicians* published in 1937, nor is he mentioned in J F Burrows' *Programmes of Magicians*.

Fred Harcourt

10 ✻ Rameses: The Forgotten Star

In Laurance Glen's 1922 book *The Magician's Road to Fame* he is shown in a poster as Ramses. This poster (now in the collection of Mike Caveney) shows how colourful the Ramses performance must have been.

There are two other well-known Rameses posters. One of them appears in the Reynolds' poster book. Both were printed by David Allen & Sons Ltd., of Belfast. Another was an eight sheet and was at one time in the Mario Carrandi collection. This was printed by Moody Bros. Although Chung Ling Soo's posters had "cornered the advertising market" so to speak, Rameses still managed to successfully promote his own show as well as the art of magic.

From my own London Palladium archive, I discovered that Rameses had been successful on the Stoll/Moss Circuit, appearing almost annually and with at least seven performances at The London Coliseum and eight performances at The Palladium, the most important of which was a Royal Variety Performance in 1914 at the height of his London career. ✤

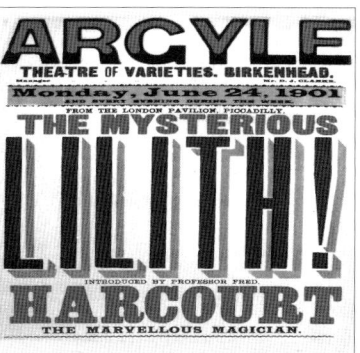

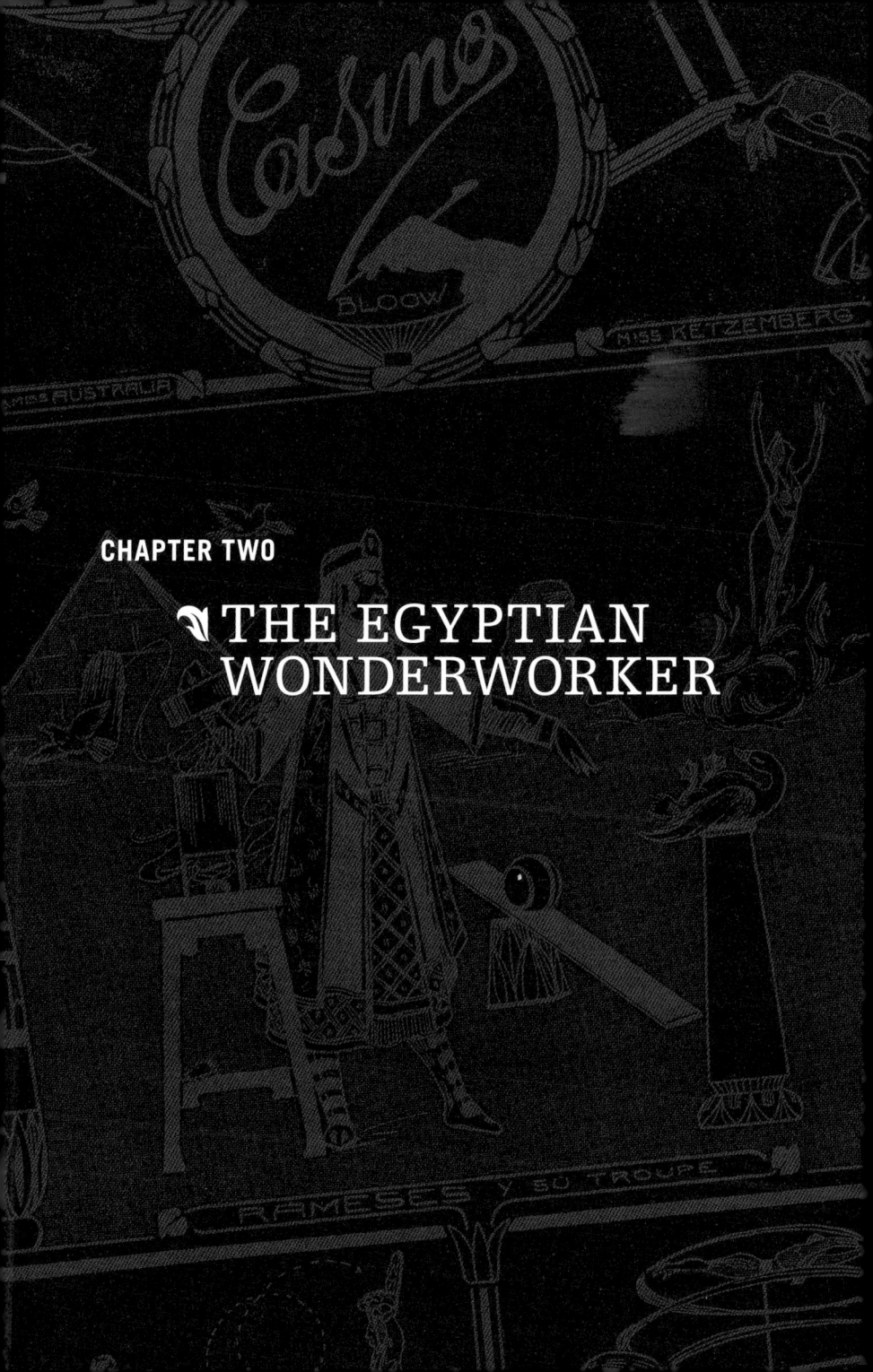

CHAPTER TWO

THE EGYPTIAN WONDERWORKER

RAMESES' FIRST RECORDED week's engagement was on October 5th 1908 at the Islington Hippodrome, London. His place on the bill was "top" at #11, and the programme stated:

> Introducing a series of the most costly, inexplicable and startling wonders ever witnessed in this country
> 1. The Mysterious Light
> 2. The Incubation
> 3. The Magic Flowers from Space
> 4. The Inexplicable
> 5 Creation of The Fire Goddess
> 6. Her Destruction
> 7. The Invisible
> 8. Transmigration
> 9. PYRO. CREMO. NECRO. REDIVI. VIVIATION.

A fascinating note in the programme also refers to "A Sliding Roof – A Novel Innovation." The Hippodrome was a theatre with a capacity of 1,800, and an interior in the style of Louis XIV. It also had ten bars!

In November of 1908, along with other top named artists of the day, Albert visited the new Gamages Magical Theatre under the aegis of the prominent Will Goldston.

In 1909, on January 25th, Marchinski appeared at the Empire Palace Theatre (later to be renamed The Olympia) on Dame Street, Dublin Ireland. *The Dublin Evening News* review had the following review:

> The place of honour on the programme at the Empire Palace theatre this week is justly allotted to 'Rameses The Egyptian Wonderworker' whose performance in his Temple of Mystery last evening afforded the spectators fifteen minutes of wonder. He fittingly opened by appearing himself seemingly from nothingness and then made a variety of articles follow his example. There was a wealth of colour light and fragrant incense about his portable temple which imparted the necessary weird air to the performance.
>
> The stage appeared all that the imagination of the European attributes to the East of mystery and magic. Rameses' swarthy assistants heightened the effect. He had the uncanny knack of producing lights at will and a convenient method of extinguishing them in his mouth. A burst of red fire beneath a cauldron containing eggs sent some pigeons flying from the interior across the stage. The onlookers eagerly sought specimens of the natural flowers that he wafted from thin air. As a sacrifice and burnt offering to his skill Rameses apparently cremated a girl dressed in a sparkling showy raiment of the East. Her subsequent presence in the auditorium allayed all fears that she had fallen victim to his necromancy.
>
> Rameses' wonders were appreciated and applauded.

Bearing in mind that this is one of Rameses' earliest known appearances, this review shows beyond all doubt his ability to "hype up" the advertising when detailing the cost of a show. Earning possibly less than £80 per week, it makes one wonder how he obtained the money to build the show, whatever the cost. Some forty-two years later his protégé Maurice Fogel would top the bill in his own right, on that very same stage.¹

Rameses' next recorded engagement was on June 21st 1909 at the 3,000 seat Liverpool Hippodrome.

Later in June of that year he appeared in Brussels at the Palais D'été. This beautiful building was originally built as an ice rink. Every spring this ice rink was transformed into a cabaret arena with

2,000 seats, where magnificent music-hall spectacles were held.

On August 30th 1909 he was at the Grand Theatre Nelson in Lancashire in the north of England. In the next two months he would appear at the Hippodrome Preston, Empire New Cross, H.M. Theatre Walsall, Hippodrome Coventry, and at the Hulme Hippodrome where *The Sphinx* would exclaim that, "Rameses'...illusions set the house in something akin to a thrill of wonder and perplexity."² In Goldston's *The Magician Monthly* a reviewer says that:

> Rameses is playing the Moss Stoll circuit with the greatest possible success. Appearing at the London Hippodrome, the Stockport Empire, the Salford Regent and, nearer home the Shepherd's Bush Empire, Frank Matcham's flagship of the 'Empire' theatres.³

16 ✳ Rameses: The Forgotten Star

And the 1909 Christmas edition of *The Performer* stated that the Rameses show had just finished a successful month's run in November at the Alhambra in Paris – a venue that had accommodated the Houdini show in April that year. Rameses was then engaged on December 16th to entertain in the Circus Carré in Amsterdam.

The following year on February 28th 1910, while appearing at the London Coliseum, Rameses caught the attention of Martin Beck, the New York Impresario. The Coliseum was the biggest theatre in central London, equal to some of the biggest stages in the US. Beck could see the great potential of Rameses' ability to "fill" the stage with his twelve-minute "whirlwind act." Beck's group of Orpheum Theatres was one of two chains that dominated big-time American entertainment. Rameses already knew that within a year of tak-

courtesy John Fisher

ing on Houdini, Beck had made good on his promise to "boom you to the top notch." Rameses also knew that Beck had arranged a successful Orpheum tour for Okito in 1908, and felt he could benefit from Beck's experience and contacts. Although Rameses already had

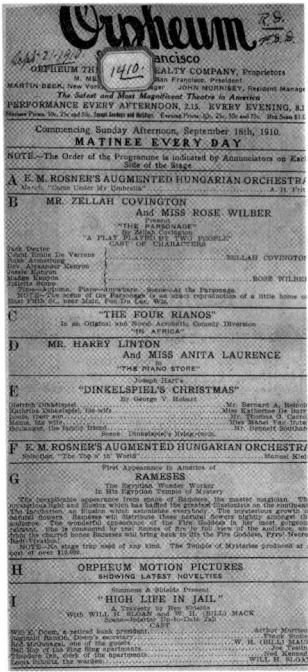

UK theatre commitments booked, negotiations began. A US tour was arranged in the early summer of that year.

In April he appeared at the Kilburn Empire. A review from Stanyon's *Magic* provides a detailed record of the Rameses show and the likely methods employed:

RAMESES, THE EGYPTIAN MYSTIC, Kilburn Empire, April, 1910

Stage setting somewhat gorgeous, practically the whole of the rear scene being arranged to represent the front of an Egyptian Temple, with a number of steps in the centre leading up to a Portico, with pillars on either side of front. Low table in centre of Portico with mirrors, arranged as in the old Sphinx Illusion, to reflect the sides of the Portico (of the same design as the rear), thus making it appear that a clear view is obtained under the table to the rear wall; an admirable arrangement for the illusion known as 'She' (shown in the course of the entertainment), inasmuch as it, to a great extent, concealed the necessity of special arrangements for the disappearance.

Appearance of Performer in Cabinet – Several attendants wheel forward the large cabinet, with curtains arranged to drop down all round on releasing cords tied to the base; shown empty, curtains dropped, pistol fired, curtains raised, and performer steps out attired in the garb of an Egyptian.

This is the only cabinet employed, and repeatedly, for the production and disappearance of persons, and in connection with which I shall suggest Change of Costume and Duplicity plays a prominent part, with the necessary traps in the base of the structure, and which appeared to be large enough to conceal one or more persons, as required.

Handkerchief from Glass Tube to Decanter — Performer places a large silk handkerchief in a tall glass cylinder standing on the back of a kind of chair, then drops cardboard tube over cylinder. He next, calls attention to an empty decanter on table on opposite side of stage, covering the mouth of the decanter with a metal cover. Handkerchief passes from the cylinder and visibly appears in the decanter.

Glass cylinder lined with a tube of clear celluloid (invisible), which was removed (carrying with it the handkerchief) within the cardboard cover. Fake with handkerchief dropped out behind chair back and the cover shown empty. Duplicate silk concealed in metal cover placed over decanter and pulled thence by a thread passing through hole in bottom of decanter and down table leg to an attendant.

Confetti to Water — Brass punch bowl shown empty, then dipped into a large box of confetti, filled, and confetti poured back again into box; filled again with confetti (?), 'top' blown off and volume of water poured out into another vessel.

Duplicate bowl containing the water may have been concealed in the box; I forget whether the box was shown afterwards or not. But this could be done were the bowl made with double sides, the water being contained all along in the intervening space. Then when dipping the bowl into the box finally, a loose tray, containing but a layer of confetti, could be pressed into the top of the bowl, a space being left for the water to be poured out.

Production of a lady with a goose from the large cabinet aforementioned — This cabinet is wheeled to the rear at the close of each production, and brought forward again as required.

Water, boiled in Cauldron, changes to Three Doves — Cauldron, size of small pail, on three short feet, placed on special table brought forward by attendants. Performer pours water into the cauldron (enough to fill it in the ordinary way), then covers the same with a deep lid. He now makes a fire of flash paper under the cauldron, after which he removes the lid, when out fly three doves.

Water passes away via the three feet into the table top. Doves contained in inner portion of lid finally left in the mouth of the cauldron.

Production of Flowers – Two trees with natural flowers produced from cone. Natural flowers, tied on stems, broken off and thrown to audience.

Performer puts on disguise, hood and cloak, completely enveloping himself.

Production of another lady from cabinet. Illusion 'She' – Lady caught screaming and forced up steps to Portico and on to table, curtain dropped all round her. Performer, breaking acid tube, fires flash paper (on front of table near bottom edge of curtain), which lights lamp, and through the flame of which he then squirts Lightning Powder from ball, or pistol with L.P. ball, held in the hand; this makes a very fiery yet harmless display. Fire out, curtain raised, when nothing but a few bones and skull are seen on table. A full explanation, illustrated with four photographs, of this illusion, with slightly different setting, will be found on pp. 72 to 74 of *Magic and Stage Illusions* (Hopkins).

Performer, under pretext of bringing on a shallow tub, rushes off the stage, his double ('She,' who has had time to pass away via trap in table and don similar disguise), returning and forthwith entering cabinet with tub. Curtains lowered while 'She' removes disguise and traps same along with the tub. Curtains raised, revealing 'She' in cabinet; the performer, who has had time to run round, appears amongst the audience in his original disguise. Another lady enters the cabinet and is changed to an old man, who forthwith retires. An excellent and very interesting show, highly applauded.[4]

At this time, there was an unfortunate preview of the legal troubles that would haunt Marchinski later in his career. In the *Stage Yearbook* for July 1910 it stated:

GEOFFREY V. RUFFELL ARTIST'S CLAIM.

The case of Geoffrey v. Ruffell's Imperial Bioscope Company, which was disposed of by His Honour Judge Woodfall in the Westminster County Court was a claim for £4. 1s., balance of salary.

For the plaintiff, it was stated that he was the proprietor of a music-hall sketch, and was engaged for a week at £16 for the Palace, Sunderland, by Mr. Rameses. Defendants were the proprietors, and plaintiff understood that they were running the hall under a "sort of partnership "Rameses paid him £3 on account, and finding that other artists were refusing to go on, he asked Mr. Ruffell's manager, Mr. Phillps, to guarantee his money. Mr. Phillips said that it would be all right, and he performed. When he went for his money he was paid £8.19s., which he was told was all that was left of what Rameses would be entitled to. He now sued the defendants, as guarantors for the balance.

The defence was that Rameses engaged all the artists, and the contract with him was produced. Phillips, it was said, had no authority to give a guarantee.

His Honour held the defendants liable, on the grounds that Phillips was in a position, in the interest of to the defendants to give the guarantee. Plaintiff and others were refusing to perform, and Phillips was anxious, in the interest of his employers, to prevent a row between the audience and the stage. He gave plaintiff judgment, with costs.

In July of 1910 Marchinski Albert was at the Poplar Hippodrome, East India Road, Poplar, London, E14 With a seating capacity of 1,830

Following the February appearance at the Coliseum, and more than likely due to distance, somewhat protracted but successful discussions had taken place, and contracts were exchanged in due course. Eventually Albert, together with his wife Rosie and his two brothers sailed from Liverpool on the Cunard ship *Lusitania*. A comparatively smooth five and a half day journey brought them to New York. The July 15th Ellis Island immigration record states that Albert was in possession of $50, his height was given as 5'7", his complexion dark, with brown hair and blue eyes. Rosie, aged thirty-two, a year younger than her husband, accompanied him, as did his two younger brothers Lesser and Abe.

In 1910 Marchinski played many cities on the Orpheum Circuit. These included, in no particular order: Seattle, San Francisco, Oakland, Kansas City, Omaha, Memphis, Minneapolis, Evansville, Sioux City, Duluth, Des Moines, Los Angeles, Lincoln, Denver, St. Paul, Salt Lake City, and Ogden. This tour ended in New Orleans.

The Beck Office had made all the necessary travel arrangements. From New York City, Marchinski took a long 2,600 mile rail journey to Denver; where, according to a report in David Price's book *Magic*, the tour opened on Monday July 31st. *The Sphinx* confirms this opening date.

It seems the fine wine had travelled well!

On Sunday afternoon September 18th the Rameses Show began appearing at the San Francisco Orpheum. This theatre was built at a cost of $1 million. Just four years after the terrible earthquake it was advertised as "The safest and most magnificent theatre in America." Rameses' billing read, "First Appearance in America: The Egyptian Wonderworker with his Temple of Mystery." With a matinee every day at 2:15 and in the evening at 8:15 in the evening the Rameses show drew rave reviews. Once again he was using the UK programme details of "No stage-traps used of any kind" and "The Temple of Mysteries produced at a cost of over $10,000." Remember there were four dollars to the pound in those days! Even with artistic licence it was still a tidy sum. He would occasionally promote his show to prospective managements by saying "We do not damage your stage as we do not use traps."

From Oakland, California, the correspondent for *Variety* wrote:

> During the twelve minutes of Rameses' act, he accomplishes about as much as the average magician in twice the time. Representing an old Egyptian temple, the act is staged in a magnificent and gorgeous manner, with flaming censers and turbaned attendants about. The rapidity with which Rameses works hails applause. In fact he might work a bit slower for effect and introduce some comedy. The most effective portion is with a curtained cabinet. From the cabinet Rameses makes his initial appearance, four others following him at different times. The feature is The Fire Goddess. A young woman is placed upon an elevated table and a hood dropped about her, surrounded by flames. The removal of the hood discloses a pile of ashes in which are placed in the cabinet together with Rameses; drawing of the curtains and his almost immediate reappearance from the rear of the audience, with the girl in his place in the cabinet. The curtains again are drawn, her reappearance from the back of the audience and replacing her in the cabinet as an old man. A commendable innovation is a silent flash of fire from the fingers instead of the startling revolver shot, favoured by the majority

of necromancers. Rameses, though not presenting anything strikingly new, goes about it in a different way, making a very interesting twelve minute turn. He was imported from Europe by the Orpheum Circuit, and is now travelling over that tour.

Raymond Stone had seen the show at his local Orpheum during October and was full of praise! Nearly thirty-five years later he described the act as follows:

> Part of it is very vivid in my memory, in spite of the fading influence of 34 years. After vanishing from a cabinet in a sheet of flame, he appeared at the back of the house; strolling rapidly down the aisle, and every few steps his hand would fly upward, with a resultant flash of fire appearing high in the air above his hand. (The house was darkened.) I have never seen before or since the auditorium use of flash paper and acid tubes. It was very definitely 'spectacular.' This was probably the program mentioned, 'the mysterious light which has baffled the greatest illusionists on the continent.'
>
> The following presents the detailed routine of 'RAMESES;' The act was presented in exactly ten minutes. Full stage. Special set. An elaborate ponderous appearing facade of an Egyptian temple. Flaming torches in urns on each side of 'Centre Door Fancy.' Several stage wise steps led up to this portal. On this raised area some of the illusions were presented (Cremation). Subdued bluish lighting. Two men and two women assistants. Costuming quite elegant.
>
> Slow curtain. A 'crash' puff of fire centre stage. As the smoke clears away there stands an Egyptian 'priest' . . . RAMESES.
>
> He steps into a curtained cabinet; another fire flash. He has departed. A 'whoop' from the rear of the house. Down the aisle he glides with long striding steps. His hand flies upward at intervals. A ball of fire results, each time. This appears several feet above his upward extended fingertips.
>
> Upon the stage once more a bandana handkerchief. From it fresh flowers are produced. These are distributed to the audience. Three eggs are tossed into a cauldron. As the last egg hits the water surface, which fills the vessel, flames leap upward. The fire subdues. Three live pigeons appear from the vessel. (Program 'The Incubation.') . . .

An outstanding impression, through the years, of Rameses, is an abundance of fire, fire and more fire.

From October 24th – 29th the Rameses show appeared at the Garrick Theatre in San Diego. Full houses ensued.

On November 6th Rameses was second to a film on the cine variety bill at the Orpheum Theatre in Salt Lake City. They played the week with no shows on Sunday, and there he was billed as *The Egyptian Necromancer*.

Prior to opening, under the weekly theatre column, the show is described. It begins with, "*Rameses the Egyptian Wonder Worker* will present ... in his *Temple of Mysteries*. Rameses is gorgeously clad in the costume of the east and his performance is along the lines of the long-established fakirs of Asia."

The bill at the Orpheum ran twice daily with a matinee at 2:15 and an evening show at 8:15, with matinee prices of 15¢, 25¢ and 50¢ and evening prices of 25¢, 50¢ and 75¢.

The theatre column lists a number of other performances including: "High Life In Jail" A travesty by Ben Shields with Wm. H. Sloan and W. H. (Bill) Mack. Mr. Zellah Covington & Miss Rose Wilber present "The Parsonage" by Mr. Covington, a play played by two people. Direct from "Yarrup" Williams & Warner, Musical Eccentriques. Inventors of the Clacophone, the Organ with a Human Voice, and Virtuosos of a Dozen Instruments, Linton & Lawrence, in "The Piano Store." The Two Racketts, in their comedy success, "Bob Fitzsimmons in Evening Dress." Harry La Belle, Athlete Extraordinaire. Orpheum Motion Pictures Greatest Novelties Orpheum Orchestra.

The report also contains an interview with Marchinski in which he denies any supernatural abilities:

When in Spokane Washington the Orpheum management held a contest. People were given a chance to try and show how the cremation illusion is done. The individual who disposed of the mystery received a prize or rather he was to receive one. No one explained it I remember a professor of astrology said that that trick was accomplished through the medium of supernatural power. Nothing could be more ridiculous. Of course I cannot tell you how I do it but it is mighty practical let me assure you of that.

Similar comments appear in a 1911 interview by *Sterling's Magic World*:

RAMESES TALKS

Rameses the Egyptian Wonder Worker has some very interesting things to say regarding magic, the kind that is used on the modern stage. 'I do not believe in the supernatural he says to me there is no such power. Certainly there is none of it in the practice of magic, for magic is practical a matter of careful study, science, careful practice and judicious application. Being a magician does not mean that you have been endowed with a gift. It means rather that you have interested yourself in the study of the forces productive of mystifying effects and that by practice you have come to be able to apply them towards some particular goal.'

Rameses counts that his best illusion is the one he calls 'The Cremation.' He says that many tried to perfect it but failed. He also believes that he is the only magician in the world who has perfected it. In addition to being a magician Rameses is a hypnotist. He is also a spiritualist to some extent; he has practiced palmistry and a few other things of this kind.[5]

Thirty-five miles or so north of Salt Lake City is Ogden Utah where Rameses also played. The theatre seated 1,750, and yet again he enjoyed a well-deserved success.

Dr. Wilson's *Magazine of Wonder* provides details of the programme and the extravagant staging:

'RAMESES, Egyptian Wonder Worker,' was at the Orpheum, Kansas City, November 28 – December 3. Act entitled, 'The Temple of Mysteries.' Stage setting mystical, awe-inspiring, superb. The performer is assisted by a company of men and women who wear rich, showy Egyptian costumes. They are as solemn and peculiar as Rameses himself. He keeps his audience guessing and gasping from the start.

The act is completely silent. Curtain rises with stage set for the appearance of Rameses from space. At the back is an altar approached by a short flight of steps. Behind this, across the back, is a drop with paintings of the sphinx and pyramids. At the sides of the altar, guarding the steps, two bronze lions support large flaming urns. Clusters of purple lights abound . . . A small pyramid is now erected on the floor of the cabinet. A door in the front of the little pyramid is closed and when opened again a woman steps out followed by a big white goose. A stand is brought to the front and what looks like a large chafing dish is placed on it. Eggs and water are put in and a fire lighted underneath. Rameses eats a few spoonfuls of the fire. Eggs and water changed to three pigeons. A woman is then bound and led, screaming, to the altar where a cloth cone is lowered over her. Fire is applied and the cloth falls. Woman has vanished and is discovered in the cabinet after curtains are drawn and opened. Several other disappearances and reappearances in the cabinet conclude the show.[6]

During the following week's appearance in Kansas City, Albert's father died on November 27th, aged fifty-four, in the UK. It was reported in the local paper that:

Rameses played under a great strain while in Kansas City, during the week of November 27. On his arriving here he found a letter from his father Philip expressing his good feeling in health and prosperity of business, but within a few hours a cablegram was received stating that his father died suddenly. This sad news could not help but depress Rameses, his wife Rosie and two brothers Lesser and Abe and it greatly interfered with their presentation of an act that required sprightliness and good humour even if it is a silent act.

The Editor writes Rameses was a modest, well-informed and most genial man to meet personally and made friends with all who had the good fortune to make his acquaintance.

The picture on the front of 'The Sphinx' for 1910 is a good likeness of Rameses as he appeared in every day costume. The one on this page is that in stage make-up, the lady beside him is Mrs. Rosie Rameses who ably assisted him throughout the entire act. Rameses has in preparation another act on new lines and which it worked out as described to me in confidence will certainly create a greater sensation than has any magic act for many years.[7]

The *Kansas City Star* spoke of his present show as follows:

Rameses, the magician, is the feature of a good bill at the Orpheum this week. It is the wonder worker's first visit to Kansas City and he is worth the while of anyone who is a patron of vaudeville. He is assisted by a company of men and women, who wear rich, showy, Egyptian costumes. They are as solemn and peculiar as Rameses himself, and added to their rhythmic actions and awe-inspiring robes is an impressive Egyptian stage setting, which makes the effect complete.

This person, Rameses, is an illusionist who-keeps his audiences guessing and gasping.[8]

Another Kansas City review, on December 7th 1910, states:

'Rameses, Egyptian wonder-worker,' with his 'Egyptian Temple of Mysteries' was at the Orpheum, this city, last week. A beautiful set-up and most artistic performance. This act conforms to the highest standards of modern magic. A description of the programme would hardly be news in England. The little details are carefully done, the audience being put in a proper state of mind for the mystery by the element of restrained wonder in the wording of the paragraph referring to the act in the theatre programme. A most inconsistent being, indeed, is he who would find fault with this entertainment. Rameses' show was enjoyed to the full by all the Kansas City magical 'bugs.'

Rameses' performances would occasionally feature seasonal adaptations. On December 25th, in St Paul Minneapolis, *The Sphinx* reported that, "One afternoon during his Minneapolis engagement he produced a 'living' Santa Claus from his magic cabinet. All children were invited on stage to receive a gift!"[9]

On December 12th, while appearing in Omaha, he witnessed a marvellous mystery performed by an inventive local magician, David P. Abbott. Albert certainly had an eye for the unusual. In this case, it was "The Talking Teakettle," an effect invented by Abbott in 1907 using induction coil technology to transmit an apparently ghostly voice into a teakettle. This was, of course, long before radio transmission was available to the masses or widely known. There were many famous magicians who visited Abbott's "House of Mystery" in Omaha, Nebraska where he gave parlor shows gratis. Abbott's greatest pleasure came from his hobby, puzzling and mystify leading performers such as Harry Kellar and Howard Thurston. Rarely did any professionals go through Omaha without paying him a visit. Blackstone, Horace Goldin, Okito and Han Ping Chien are just a few who knew him and who were his guests. Albert snapped up the opportunity to meet Abbott, too, and see his new wonder, the talking teakettle.

In January of 1911, Rameses wrapped up his tour, performing in Milwaukee, Chicago, St. Louis, and Indianapolis. On January 1st he was at the Majestic Theatre Milwaukee. The highly successful Orpheum Tour closed on February 12th in New Orleans. Marchinski and company sailed from New York to Liverpool on March 8th 1911.

On April 3rd 1911, the Rameses show began starring in a regular week of variety at the new 2,300 seat London Palladium. These appearances would be the beginning of another successful circuit of the London theatres as well as the rest of the UK. He performed at The Palladium with the Kauffman Troupe of Lady Cyclists, the actress Miss Valli Valli, and Drama "Heard in Camera" with popular west-end actors Eric Mayne and Miss Frances Dillon.

prepared the house for occupation. It needed to be fully redecorated and refurnished to a very high standard.

A large group of performers organized a plan known as "The Noble Six Hundred" whereby each person could contribute £2.10.0. (equivalent to £994 today) in order to pay off the mortgage of £1,400 (£557,200). The generosity of the theatrical profession knew no bounds and within a few short months the large sum had been raised.

A large board was erected in the home that remains to this very day, detailing all the six-hundred names. Both Albert and Mrs. Rameses are listed as two of the "Noble Six Hundred." Though Rameses was earning around £70.00 a week at this time, £2.10.0 was still a substantial donation. The home is still going strong and is still funded by The Grand Order of Water Rats, relying on individual bequests and funds derived annually by the televising of The Royal Variety Performance helping those less fortunate artists or their dependants.

Albert and Mrs. Rameses were in the good company of other famous magical names who also made donations, among them Carl Hertz, Horace Goldin, Owen Clark, Servais le Roy, Walford Bodie, Pharos, Chris Van Bern and Sydney Lee.

Rameses continued working in 1912, performing at the Canning Town Imperial Theatre, the Shoreditch Olympia Theatre, and the Willesden Hippodrome.

Soon after, Rameses would take his show on a seventeen-week tour of South Africa. *The Magic Mirror* listed the theatres for the forthcoming Rameses South Africa Tour. These included: The Grand Theatres of South Africa, The New Grand Theatre Jo'burg, Bijou Jo'burg, Apollo Germiston SA, Grand Theatre Pretoria, Grand Theatre Pietermaritzburg, Grand Theatre Port Elizabeth, and Grand Theatre Capetown.[12]

Only a decade after The Boer War, and in the intervening years, Sandow and Cinquevalli, Ada Reeve and George Robey, Eugene Stratton had all been booked to entertain South African audiences. Harry Ctadel, a shrewd and experienced English pioneer, primarily a cinema man, bought the Tivoli and ran it as a variety house. Rameses show was one of his earliest successful productions.

By April 10th *The Cape Times* newspaper for Cape Town South Africa reviewed the show with this report:

RAMESES A WIZARD OF EGYPT

The Tivoli Theatre was packed with a big crowd last night for the South African debut of 'Rameses, the Egyptian Mystic' who promised bewildering illusions and all sorts of inexplicable wizardry.

It was quite clear by the enthusiasm shown at the end of the evening that the latest entertainment shown for Tivoli patrons is quite to their liking.

Rameses and his wonders of magic proved his worth in a short scene of things inexplicable according to normal codes. Several vanishing tricks and good conjuring tricks figured in the proceedings and Rameses himself instead of walking on in the manner of an ordinary individual, appeared suddenly behind the curtains of an apparently empty palanquin like a proper man of magic!

The stage of The Tivoli is not quite large enough to accommodate the scenery in such a manner as to retain a sense of mystery. For the whole act is set in a sort of temple of Mystic Rites. There are brazen bowls of flame and priest attired in all the gorgeousness of Egyptian apparel. Rameses himself is made up to resemble one of the most noted of the ancient kings of that name and both in the appearance and in the mysteries is reminiscent of the far off days of the obsolete dynasties.

...The whole act is extremely sensational, and is certain to prove a great attraction.[13]

While it was reported in the magical press that Rameses & Company went to South Africa for a "twenty week" tour, records show that within seventeen weeks he was back in the UK appearing at The Palladium once again. He appeared on the following bill: 1 *Overture*, 2 *Jean Robb*, 3 *Daisy Dormer*, 4 *The Four Charles*, 5 *Whit Cunliffe*, 6 *Arthur Bourchiers Co in "Striking Home"* 8 *Gobert Belling Animal Speciality Extraordinaire*, 9 *Anna Dorothy*, 10 *RAMESES*, 11 *Collins Troupe*, 12 *Tom Edwards*, 13 *Karno's "Perkins in Paris" with Albert Bruno*.

The poster for his July 22nd performance at the Kilburn Empire Theatre billed the event as, "His first London engagement since returning home from South Africa."

On August 19th 1912, Rameses performed at the Burnley Palace, which had opened in December of 1907; was built at a cost of £13,000; and would seat 2,200 people.

On September 2nd London was to gain another new theatrical venue: the Chiswick Empire. Once again of Matcham design, the theatre had a capacity of 1,948. The interior decor was mainly electric blue and terracotta and, very advanced for its time, it had a sliding roof.

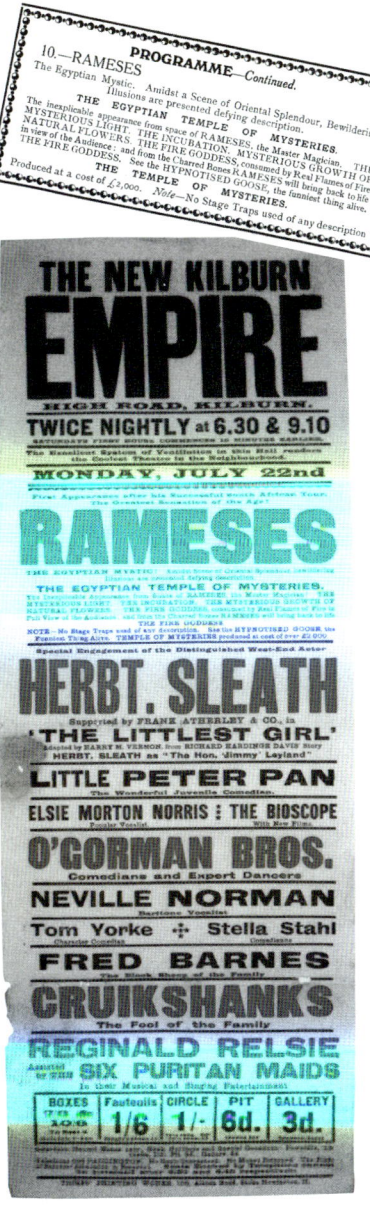

The Egyptian Wonderworker ✹ 33

In the September issue of *The Magician Monthly* for 1912, Goldston describes how Rameses & Company handled a significant technical difficulty at the Chiswick Empire:

> We were present at the first performance at the Chiswick Empire, and were glad to find that a magical show was one of the star turns. It was supplied by Rameses the Egyptian magician. The act was a most effective one, full of light and colour and crowded with mysterious happenings. Halfway through it, however, there was an unfortunate accident. Some of the scenery collapsed doubtless owing to the hurry and confusion incidental to a first night performance. The results might have been very serious, for there were burning braziers on the stage at the time. But Rameses and his assistants were alert to the occasion. In a moment or two they had restored the scenery to its place and were continuing the act. Congratulations to them. And congratulations to Oswald Stoll.[14]

A week later, on September 9th yet another Matcham theatre opened across town. It was the Wood Green Empire Theatre, with a capacity of 1,840. Just like the Chiswick show the previous week, each patron received a silk programme. Rameses was paid £50 for the week's engagement.

It was at this very theatre six years later, that Rameses' colourfully clad counterpart Chung Ling Soo would present his final, tragic performance of the bullet catch. Thirty-two years later still, Rameses' protégé Maurice Fogel would successfully duplicate the dangerous Bullet Catch on the same stage.

On September 23rd Rameses appeared at The Coliseum #7 alongside Marie Novello, with the legendary Sarah Bernhardt at the top of the bill.

A review from this period describes one of a handful of important new additions to Rameses' repertoire:

PALACE AND HIPPODROME, BURNLEY Sat August 17th 1912'

> ... In the old days necromancers were believed to be the interpreters of the Gods; nowadays we know that is all trickery, but with all our modern learning we are still capable of being thoroughly mystified. This Rameses is at the top of his profession and his feats are performed with an Eastern weirdness and silence which are decidedly in keeping with the character assumed. After tricks with a handkerchief and tinsel turning to water, the audience on Monday were shown a mysterious ball which rolled up and down a plank at command without visible agency...

In the popular newspaper *Tit-Bits* for January 25th 1913 there was a full page interview called "MAGICIANS OF THE METROPOLIS: A special interview with Leading London Entertainers." This included, "# 5 RAMESES THE EGYPTIAN MYSTIC WHO WORKS HIS WONDERS IN SILENCE." The interview provides a glimpse into Marchinski's good-humoured and worldly personality:

RAMESES

The Great Egyptian Mystic, received the representative of Tit-Bits upon the Coliseum stage where he was rehearsing his new illusion, and although he gave him a great deal of copy he declined to disclose even for the benefit of our readers, the secret of the trick 'The Goddess of the Nile' of which more anon.

The scene, with its mighty columns and its Egyptian architecture seemed like the entrance to some vast Egyptian

RAMESES.

temple at Luxor, and the make-up of the magician himself is a faithful reproduction, as regards robe and headdress, of that of the great Pharaoh himself.

When You Hear The East A Calling

'What do you desire of me' asked Rameses, in a voice which might, have belonged to one of the Egyptians themselves.

And falling into the atmosphere of the scene, the T.B. man remarked. 'I would learn of thee of the secrets of the mighty East.'

Then Rameses threw off the ancient air and became quite modern as he quoted Kipling 'When you hear the East a-calling, well, you don't need anything else.'

'The East, as represented by you upon the stage' said the T.B. philosopher, ' is the thing that has caused me to need a great deal more, and that is some information about your illusions and about yourself, I put your illusions first. I hope you don't mind?'

'Not at all' said Rameses. 'Which of my illusions has fascinated you the most?'

'Cremation' said Tit-Bits boldly.

'Ah, that, I think is perhaps my most effective one. And it is really founded on a legend which has been translated from an Egyptian papyrus.'

No Traps, No Doubles

'If you can find space to say so in your interview, I wish you would emphasize one or two points about my performance. They may not be self-evident, but please walk about the stage yourself and see that I speak truly. In no trick or illusion are any stage traps used, and I pledge, you my word of honour that we do not indulge in doubles.

THE MAGIC BALL TRICK

Moreover, as regards my wonderful magic ball, which I have greatly much improved and which runs up and down an inclined plane defying the laws of gravity, it can be examined by yourself or by any member of the audience during the performance. I defy anybody to detect its secret, and I have added something which no other trick of the same kind — and there are imitations — possesses. At the end of my experiments with this ball it runs right to the top of the inclined plane and jumps into space.' And Rameses there and then demonstrated that it did so.

'This head-dress,' he remarked as he took it off and set it on one side, 'is very heavy. It is an exact reproduction of the head-dress of Rameses II, and the jewel in the centre was originally purchased by me from a jeweller in Cranbourn Street, who told me that it formed the buckle of a girdle worn by Mrs. Brown Potter.'

A Funny Story

One hardly expected so staid and austere looking a magician as Rameses to condescend to tell a funny story, but he certainly possesses a fund of humour unsuspected by those who see his show, because all his tricks and illusions are performed in absolute silence. No word is spoken on the stage from start to finish, and the development of the trick has to be closely watched by the spectators it is their eyes only which are deceived their hearing is not led astray.

'The funniest experience,' he said, 'which I remember was in regard to the hypnotized goose. You know that it is possible to hypnotize a goose, and it forms a part of one of my illusions where the goose is hypnotized and white doves are produced from a cauldron steaming over a gas fire.

By the way I had to prove to the satisfaction of the Society of The Prevention of Cruelty to Animals as I know that conjurers with bird tricks have also had to do though the pigeons suffered no pain or injury. But to return to the goose. It was in Wakefield, just before Christmas, that I put forth the challenge that no one could bring a goose which I could not hypnotize. If they succeeded in doing so — I would pay £100.

Well that night the theatre was a sight. Lots of them were keeping geese for their Christmas dinner, they brought the birds all to be hypnotized with the sporting chance of making £100 as a Christmas — box. One by one the geese, with identifying labels tied round their necks, were handed across the footlights, and one by one I hypnotized until there were some seventy or eighty of them lying in rows upon the stage! The house simply rocked with laughter. It was like giant poulterer's shop.

Then I proceed to wake the geese up and they waddled and quacked – by the way do geese quack? Anyhow, they made curious noises they ran about the stage. But there were two geese that I could not dis–hypnotize. I tired my best and in the end I had to push them off into the wings sound asleep and go on with another trick. Of course the challenge had been that I would hypnotize them not dis-hypnotize (sic) them or I should have been a tight corner over that £100. All the alive and kicking geese having been returned to their rightful owners I suggested that the possessors of the two sleepy birds should come the stage door after the show for them which they did. I wondered what I could say to them for the geese were still fast asleep but they saved me any trouble by remarking "We had seen you before we liked your show and so we thought we'd help you by doping them these geese and as a matter of fact we so loaded these two birds up with gin that they were drunk literally as drunk as owls and as a matter of fact did not return to a state of sobriety for four and twenty hours.'

Indian Fakir Tricks

'The question,' said Rameses, when our representative had finished laughing 'has been asked me more than once if there is any reasonable explanation of some of the famous Indian tricks, and if I think that there is. They are based upon much simplicity and a large amount of artfulness upon the part of the magician. There is of course, the basket trick, which has been frequently exposed.

It consists of the shape of the basket enabling the person contained therein to curl himself up in such a manner that a sword can be passed through apparently any portion of the wicker-work without injury to him, and the basket appears to be quite empty. There is another basket trick, from which the boy placed in it disappears and reappears behind the circle of spectators where sitting round but that, of course is done with a double bottomed basket and the use of a double. As to the famous rope trick; where a rope is thrown over the branch of a very tall tree – or over a beam between two palm trees, and up which a boy swarms and disappears into space, I believe the solution of that to be, although I have never seen it done myself, that with the blazing Indian sun beating down upon the yellow sand the audience is only able to see up for a certain distance, in blinding rays of 'Old Sol' dazzling and bewildering their eyes, with the result that after the boy has climbed a certain distance, although he is still clinging to the rope, he is invisible to them.'

The Mango Trick Exposed

'But the trick which is the chef-d'oeuvre is undoubtedly the growing mango tree, and it is the cleverest fraud ever conceived. It is generally performed on the sand outside a bungalow, and the effect of the trick is that the Indian squats down upon the ground and, after covering the sand in front of him with a brilliantly coloured silk shawl, removes it and shows a tiny mango tree – a mere twig with a few leaves – starting to grow. He covers it again, and it has grown a little more; and again, and again, and again, until it is a tall tree – bearing; a ripe mango upon it. The explanation is simplicity itself. Overnight the Indian has secretly dug a little pit in the sand, and into this he sinks a long tin cylinder, something like a coffee can. In this he places the full-grown mango tree attached to a disc of thick cork the circumference of the cylinder. The top of the mango tree just reaches the surface of the sand on which he is seated. When he covers it with his silk shawl he scoops away with his fingers a little of the covering sand, with the result that the few green leaves on the top of the tree become visible. Then he takes a pitcher of water and waters the plant to make it grow.

Obviously, the more water which he pours into the cylinder the more it forces the cork up and the more the tree fixed to this thick base of cork, rises to the surface. He continues to scoop away the sand as it is pushed up by the water, until at last the full grown tree, with the ripe mango on it is exposed.'

The Goddess Of The Nile

'And now for my new trick of my own which I do not propose to explain.

There are two tanks upon the stage one 'up stage' and the other 'down' nearer the footlights and I prove there is no connection between the two. The lower one contains water of a somewhat murky appearance, a little milky while the upper one is clear water. Into the clear water descends 'The Goddess of the Nile,' and immediately that begins to become turbid and cloudy while the water in the lower tanks gradually clears. The Goddess has gone from the top tank and is seen reclining in the bottom one. I think it will startle any audience.'

The Living Mummy Trick

'And now before you go my little Mummy trick for your readers. Tell a man to stand up straight his hands by his sides, his right shoulder and his right foot flush against the wall, and then let him bring his left until it is side by side with his right foot as if he were standing to attention on parade and he will fall over from the wall to the floor as it if he were a mummy.'

The Tit-Bits man tried it and found that Rameses was quite right!

A second tour was arranged by Beck, and on March 9th 1913 Rameses left Southampton and sailed for Buenos Aires, Argentina.[15] The French magazine *L'Illusioniste* says that Rameses performed at the Casino in Buenos Aires, Argentina. The casino where Rameses &

Company appeared was the first music hall in the country and became undoubtedly the greatest venue for live entertainment. Their appearance at the casino commencing March 28th was a tremendous success. In July Rameses and his seven-person company appeared in the Casino in Montevideo Uruguay. Later that month, he brought his company to the Palace Theatre in Rio de Janeiro for the remainder of that successful season.

On June 21st "Albert Rameses" along with his wife Rosie (although the manifest called her

Rosa) arrived back in New York from Rio de Janeiro on the 1,500-ton vessel *Vandyck*.

The manifest details are given as "touring." Martin Beck of Times Square was their contact. Beck had obviously prepared another Orpheum Tour.

In September of 1913 Rameses & Company were again in Salt Lake City. The ad read:

AT THE ORPHEUM

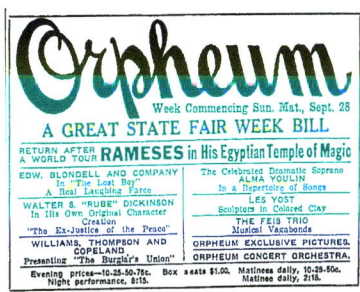

For the State Fair week the management of the Orpheum offers a great bill topped by that famous mystic, Rameses & Co. To the four corners of the earth has Rameses travelled with his Egyptian Temple of Magic and all corners has he astonished audiences with his weird skill in making things to appear as they are not. No less interested were the audiences of Tasmania than those of the London halls. No less perplexing and fascinating in his performance than when he toured America before – indeed he has added to and perfected his offering until now it is little short of perfection. With rare skill as a showman but greater deftness as an illusionist, Rameses makes his allotted time on stage fairly reek with thrills. His scenery is most elaborate and beautiful. There is one fact that is most noteworthy and that is that not one trap door of any sort is used in his entire act.

Yet again Albert was in the news, once again condemning the practice of Spiritualism."There is no such thing as Magic, Mind Reading or Spiritualism. All Fakes- Rameses" was the headline:

> 'There is no such thing as magic, no such things as second sight or mind reading or thought transference; there is nothing but humbug and fakery in Hindoo mysticism and I challenge any spiritualist or medium to show me any trick or trickery done by him or her that I haven't done in the open or cannot do. And I will repeat that challenge

as often as they desire and meet the best of them under their own conditions and not only do things they do but things that they cannot do and without any spirits, either.'

This sweeping assertion was made by Rameses the magician now working at the Orpheum. Rameses himself, who learned many of the tricks he performs from the magicians of Egypt, where be says the best in the world are to be found, does things that are incredible to the naked eye. But every trick he performs is simple 'when you know how.' That, he declares, is all there is to the best work of the best medium that ever cajoled a duped circle and in his list of fakirs he includes palmists, astrologers and mediums alike.

'Palladino, who fooled the so called savants of two continents,' he went on 'was found out. John Slater, the American, was found out. It's the same with all of them – tricks, tricks, that anyone can do who devotes the time and attention to that sort of thing. We do those things on the stage all the time. There they are too common to be worthwhile any more.'

'Don't you suppose if I went into a dark room and surrounded myself with a lot of gammon and fakery I could be the greatest medium that ever lived, if I merely made a girl go up in flames and then brought her to life from her own ashes: Yet I do that twice a day on a stage, and it is only one of a number of tricks to amuse the public. So divest a medium of his or her embellishments and mystery and put that same medium out in the open and what would happen? The medium's wonders would be so silly and so simple that the present dupes would be the first to laugh at them!

How about the celebrated fakirs of India? I was asked.

What do they do that we cannot do? They make a man and a woman disappear yes. I do the same with a woman. They make flowers grow before your eyes. So do I, and I give you the flowers to prove it. They make a boy climb a rope thrown into the air and disappear. Well, did you ever try to look up into the air on a bright, sunny day. How far

> There is No Such Thing as Magic, Mind Reading or Spiritualism, All Fakes
> —Rameses

can you see, especially if you are facing the sun. Take that same sun in the tropics, where it blazes still more intensely, and your line of vision is lower. How do you know the boy bas disappeared? He has merely gone out of your range of vision, that's all. I never yet have seen a person who has actually witnessed these so called feats; they have always heard of some one else who has. Buncombe, (sic) all of it.'[16]

By November Rameses was performing at the Orpheum in St. Paul. *The Magic Wand* describes Rameses' performance of "The Talking Teakettle:"

Rameses is the reputed owner of a spirit. She was once an Egyptian Princess but now in spirit form dwells in a kettle. Rameses keeps the kettle in his drawing room and if the spirit – and the current – is willing, messages are transmitted via the spout of the kettle.[17]

The following year Rameses was back in the UK and appeared at the Glasgow Playhouse. In an article in *Sterling's Magic World*, entitled "Between Ourselves," the reviewer wrote:

Most people are familiar with the kettle singing on the hob but how many have really heard the kettle singing intelligently. Rameses is playing this week at the Glasgow Playhouse and has achieved apparently the impossible in training not only an ordinary tea kettle, but an ordinary oriental vase to 'sing' out scotch ballads or ragtime ditties (at the desire of an audience) sufficiently audible for the largest theatres. A private demonstration was given recently a The London Palladium with marked success. Magic it is, but new magic.[18]

In the *Goldston Annual of Magic* for 1915/16 a "talking kettle" – based on the induction coil principle – is fully detailed, but it is not known

which method Rameses used.[19] It can be presumed that it was the Abbott apparatus, as it is unlikely that Marchinski would have had access to the necessary equipment to make one for himself (as he had done with Servais LeRoy's "Stolen Jam" illusion). However it is known that Rameses presented the "talking kettle" at the *First Grand All Magical Séance of the Magicians' Club* at Casa Rosa, Glebe Place, and Chelsea Street on Sunday Evening April 25th 1915.

Later Maurice Fogel would also perform a variant on this effect. In his *Spook Party*, one of the attractions was a "Talking Bucket." Bobby Bernard and Philip "Jake" Jacobs were the unseen assistants in this, using a simple thread to lift the handle that would drop and make a clatter. Once for yes and twice for no.

On February 8th 1914 Rameses entertained at the Ladies Night for Goldston's Magicians' Club:

> On the 8th inst., the third Ladies' Night was held, and despite an exceedingly wet evening, by 7-30 the room was packed to its utmost capacity. Mr. Harry Houdini was in the chair, supported by Oswald Williams, Rameses, Cecil Lyle, Harry Day, Sydney Lee, Will Goldston and Stanley Collins.

Later that month Rameses & Company were at the Balham Hippodrome with more new illusions:

RAMESES AT THE BALHAM HIPPODROME

REVIEW From a resplendent canopy, previously shown empty by a lady assistant, Rameses makes his appearance in the striking surroundings of a gorgeous Egyptian Temple. A neatly worked flight of a handkerchief, from a glass cylinder to a position between two other knotted silks, opens the performance, the introduction being quickly followed by the transformation of a bowlful of glittering gold, to water, in which goldfish disport themselves. Rameses next introduces the ball on the plank, the trick being shown with a high degree of finish.

A pyramid is now erected on a platform, and from it the principal assistant is again produced, together with a goose. The highly trained descendant of the 'birds that saved Rome,' permits himself to be 'mesmerized,' awakening from his trance at the same moment that a number of doves take flight from a receptacle a few moments before proved to be empty. The introduction of what figure, on the programme as 'Pyro-Cremo-Necro-Redivivation,' proves to be a form of the illusion 'Cremation.' which to the accompaniment of much red fire, is a telling effect. 'Vril,' the mysterious automaton, apparently actuated from an induction coil of prodigious dimensions, goes through a number of queer antics, and a series of smartly worked quick changes completes the illusionary act.

Rameses works in a carefully studied style, presenting his effects with commendable attention to detail, and as a result, the performance goes with a swing from start to finish, deservedly obtaining well-merited applause.[20]

"Vril," it should be said, was in effect an assistant suitably dressed in a Pierrot costume and hooked up to an impressive looking "control box" with all the wires and mechanics to make it look as though it was a "robot" under the complete control of Rameses. I recall being told by Maurice Fogel about "lead boots." I foolishly never thought

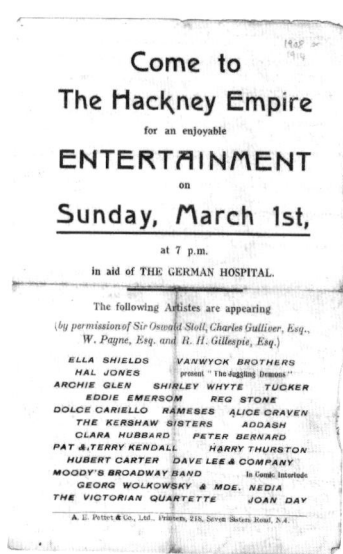

then to ask more about what he meant by the subject, but it was obvious that the assistant would be wearing this heavy footwear enabling him to bend in all directions without toppling over.

Another Maurice, this time Maurice Blackman, also a kind member of The Magic Circle, told me that his grandfather, a metal-worker, made some "special legs" for Rameses. Whether the effect used a puppet or a person suitably dressed is only speculation at this point.

During this time, and to this day, artists were often asked to appear for a deserving charity, and on Sunday March 1 1914 Rameses & Company obliged with a Charity Performance at the Hackney Empire in aid of the German Hospital. With a superb bill the 1,900 seats were sold out in no time.

Rameses was back at the London Palladium for a week commencing on Monday March 16th. The show went as follows: 1 *Overture*, 2 *Cavalotti Bros*, 3 *Sammy Shields*, 4 *Little Freddie Haskin quick*

PROGRAMME—Continued.

8. RAMESES.

The Magic of the Pharaohs outdone, return after a World Tour of the Master of Mystery. The Magician from the Orient in **THE EGYPTIAN TEMPLE OF SPLENDOUR** wherein the secrets of this age are disclosed. SEE the inexplicable and puzzling appearance of this uncanny Eastern Wizard. Such seemingly impossible happenings as a globe defying the Laws of Gravitation. Incubation: producing live birds from cinders. The Building of the Pyramids and their Secrets. The Hypnotized Goose. The Wonder of Life. Scientists amazed. The Complex appearance of the Goddess of Fire. PYRO-CREMO-NECRO-REDIVIVATION. The Mystery of Mysteries. A Beautiful Woman consumed by Fire, Rameses, from the charred Remains, brings her back to life in full view of the audience. The Management guarantee no Stage Traps are used. RAMESES presents the Query of the Universe, VRIL, the Acme of the Uncanny. Is VRIL Human, Mechanical, or a being under the **ABYSMAL POWER OF RAMESES?** Remarkable, Mysterious, Scientific, Weirdly Exciting. Sensational.

change, 5 *The Westminster Singers*, 6 *Intermission*, 7 *The Follies*, 8 *RAMESES*, 9 *Ruth Vincent*, 10 *Ernie Lottinga*, 11 *Phil Ray*, 12 *Hetty King Barclay Gammon.*

Following the regular Monday variety opening night, Marchinski would receive a great honour for someone of such humble beginnings: a royal audience.

A ROYAL VARIETY PERFORMANCE

It was this much-heralded show that set the seal on the successful future of The Palladium. With a precedent of sometimes bawdy music halls, the royal audience confirmed for the general public that they too could attend "variety" performances without guilt. The line up was as follows: *The national anthem was sung by Ruth Vincent*, 1 *The Poluskis*, 2 *Jackson's Sixteen English Dancers*, 3 *Coram*, 4 *Boganny's*, 5 *Clarice Mayne and That (J W.Tate)*, 6 *Sammy Shields*, 7 *Sir George Alexander presents "A Social Success,"* 8 *Phyllis Bedells*, 9 *Fred Emney*, 10 *George Robey*, 11 *RAMESES*, 12 *National Anthem.*

The Standard stated in their report:

THE KING AND QUEEN AT THE PALLADIUM.
A MERRY PROGRAMME

Hardly were the royal party conformably settled in their box, after listening to a verse of the National Anthem and bowing in response to hearty cheering, when another of those unpleasant incidents occurred which of late seem inevitable at royal visits to places of amusement. A wild woman, evidently one of the following of Mrs. Pankhurst, stood up in the dress circle and shouted something about 'torture in prison.'

A storm of hisses and shouts of protest from the huge audience of some 3,000 people soon made her utterances inaudible, and approving cheers greeted the policeman who grasped the woman and disappeared with her. It was subsequently ascertained that the woman was allowed to go free.

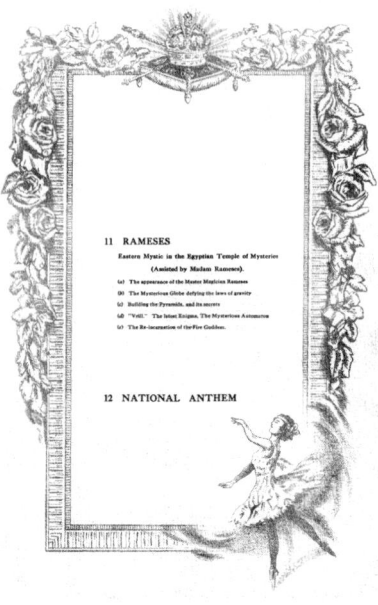

During the minute or so of disturbance the Queen played with the flowers in front of her and the King turned over the leaves of the beautifully printed programme, and seemed to call the attention of his cousin, Princess Dagmar, who was of the party, to the excellent photographs of himself and Queen Mary. It was also noticed that the Queen's gown was of crushed strawberry colour, matching her hat, which had a high crimson plume, and that dark furs were thrown back from her shoulders. Princess Mary had on a bright red coat, and the Danish Princess was apparently in black, with sombre furs. There were great bundles of flowers wherever it was possible to put them in the royal box, which was also hung with light silken draperies, and the front of the stage had a wide bank of many hued blossoms.[22]

Despite this political confrontation, the performance was a success for Rameses and the other performers.

The following day all the reviews were positive. *The Standard* reported as follows:

> Some Egyptian conjuring was the final turn in the programme – very wonderful and watched with profound interest by Princess Mary – and then the National Anthem from the orchestra, and the King and Queen bowed farewell greeting to their loyal lieges.[23]

The Referee reported:

> The final turn was given by 'Rameses, The Egyptian Mystic' one of whose many amazing feats namely the hypnotising of a goose and the subsequent producing a flock of pigeons from a boiling saucepan was included in his act only after the Queen had been thoroughly assured that there was no danger to the birds concerned.[24]

The Stage newspaper said, "Rameses introduced a number of bewildering illusions staged in magnificent style."

The Magic Wand for June had this to say:

> The interest taken in the art of magic by members of the Royal Family is a matter of common knowledge. It has been stated on good authority that His Majesty King George enjoys witnessing a good conjuring performance as well as anything, and it will be remembered that the late King Edward frequently sought the aid of clever magicians – notably Charles Bertram – to entertain his guests. At a command performance within recent memory, David Devant, that arch-wizard of St. George's Hall, was one of the shining lights, and later, at the request of Queen Alexandra, he provided a complete magical act. The illusionist, Rameses, with his magnificent Eastern setting, was one of the entertainers at the last vaudeville performance officially visited by our present King, and Queen and, until recently, it was not an uncommon sight to witness one or other of the young Princes roaming round a well-known conjuring store. In view of the advance magic has made in recent years, and its undoubted appeal to cultured people, conjuring might, perhaps, be described as a Royal hobby-at any rate, it may safely be stated to be one of them.[25]

Other than a Royal diary entry stating, "part of it was amusing" there is, sadly, no correspondence within The Royal Archives relating to this show. However over £2,000 was raised for this deserving charity. A princely sum indeed!

As with all Royal Charity performances there was a plethora of programme sellers. Some well-known names of the day were Yvonne Arnaud, Gladys Cooper, Cecily Courtneidge, and Phyllis Monkman.

One should appreciate the great honour it was for Albert and Rose Marchinski to appear before Royalty so early in their career. Today one can easily become blasé about "appearing before Royalty" but in that time, the honour was even greater. I am sure nerves played a role in giving Rameses' an edge over his rivals following this very great accolade.

Between engagements on Sunday March 22nd, Rameses, Lesser, and Albert Simmons paid a visit to Will Goldston's Magicians' Club,

no doubt to recount Royal stories from the previous week's engagement. Always with an eye for publicity, from then on he was often billed as *Rameses – The Royal Magician*.

Back to the real world, on May 4th, he began appearing twice nightly at Camberwell Palace.

The Magicians' Club First Annual Supper and Ball took place on May 4th 1914. This was held at the Hotel Cecil. On this special night the cabaret was extra special in that Harry Houdini, Charles Morritt, Carl Hertz, Stanley Collins, as well as Chris van Bern and The Zomahs all appeared in the gala entertainment. Rameses was also billed to appear.

The Aldershot Review gives more information about the "Vril" illusion that Rameses presented on August 31st at the Hippodrome:

> ...the greatest mystery...entitled 'Vril." A figure is dressed as a Pierrot, whether man or doll probably no one can tell, is placed on a platform and an electric battery is connected with cables and the figure begins to move assuming a sitting position without any support and executes various other movements.[26]

The idea of the name for this illusion came from Edward Bulwer-Lytton's 1871 science fiction novel *The Coming Race* in which "Vril"

50 ❋ Rameses: The Forgotten Star

is a powerful and mysterious electric substance. Marchinski's levitation effect took inspiration from H. Rider Haggard's 1905 gothic novel *Ayesha: the Return of She*, in particular, the description, "She never dies. She changes, that is all. As the wind blows... so she comes and goes,... on the earth, or beyond it..."

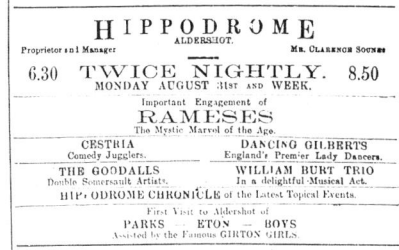

1914 August 31st – Aldershot Hippodrome

In the late 1890's, Frederick Eugene Powell 'The Master of Modern Magic' was presenting "She," the apparent burning to ashes of a beautiful woman in full view of the audience. "She" was taken from the H. Rider Haggard novel of the same name. Rameses continued with this literary theme by using "Ayesha" as the title for *his* floating lady, in the same way as Harcourt had done with "Lilith" the female demon associated with wind.

The Magic Wand issue in December 1914 announced Rameses' first performance of "Ayesha." [27]

Rameses' new additions immediately gained the attention of reviewers. Reporting on his performance on February 22nd 1915 at the Holborn Empire Theatre, Goldston's *The Magician Monthly* says:

> Rameses is causing considerable wonderment with his Egyptian act introducing 'Vril' experiments and his great levitation. Rameses has a well-planned show and knows how to get over the footlights; effectiveness of setting and well trained assistants help to make up a very fine turn. Rameses is well booked and we have little doubt that while his show is kept to its present level it should remain so. [28]

The Egyptian Wonderworker

Within a year he was back again in Argyll Street, this time for a two weeks engagement. A second review by the same magazine gives further details:

> The piece de resistance is the remarkable effect which is obtained by the application of electricity to a figure dressed as a Pierrot. And the effect is too weird for mere description to do it justice. One is left wondering and guessing, for whether the figure is human, or in very truth what it seems to be, merely a lay figure, the difficulty of causing it to bend back from the knees until the body is at right angles, supported in no way whatever, is obvious enough, whether one regards it as human or not; but when we are faced with the next problem, that of Rameses standing on the breast of the unsupported figure, well, speaking for ourselves, we frankly gave it up. We are told that 'Vril' is the force employed (taken from the book "The Coming Race," by Lord Lytton). 'Vril' being a highly concentrated invisible electric fluid, possessing a thousand times greater activity than any form of electricity now known, which, of course, explains everything, except how it's done. We cordially recommend a visit to Rameses, to all who wish to give their thinking apparatus a spring clean; it will need it, if it is to discover the mystery of 'Vril.' [29]

Will Goldston in reviewing the act remarked that:

> ...his turn is one of the most popular of the variety theatre bookings. He gets in his act the atmosphere of mystery almost terror in rare degree, and his magical effects are instinct with drama and quick appeal to the emotions. [30]

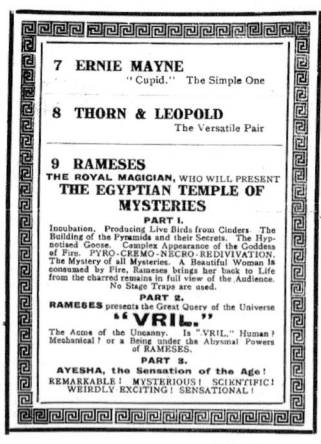

courtesy Mike Caveney

On April 25th 1915 Rameses & Company appeared at Goldston's Magicians' Club on a very special occasion. It was the first Grand Séance. Will Goldston appeared recreating his Carl Devo act, others on the star studded show included Carlton, Lewis Davenport, Goldin, Carl Hertz, Leipzig, Morritt, Chung Ling Soo, and Zomah.

On August 8th Mr & Mrs. Rameses attended another special Goldston Magicians' Club gathering to honor Frank Van Hoven. The following night he was at the Holborn Empire for the week of August 9th.

1915 September 16th *The Performer* stated: "The Egyptian Mystic is a veritable Sphinx for secrecy and he must be piling up pyramids of money."

In the September 1915 issue of Goldston's *Magician Monthly* it was announced that, "The Committee of the Magicians' Club propose to elect not more than fifty "Life Members of the Club at the subscription of £3.3s 0d (£3.30p)." Rameses quickly responded and would join the ranks of Harry Houdini, David Devant, Chris van Bern, Frank Van Hoven, Carlton, Lewis Davenport, Ernest Sewell, Stanley Collins, and Will Goldston amongst others.

On November 15th 1915 he was contracted to appear at the Bolton Hippodrome. Such was the guarantee of his success that instead of a salary he was contracted to appear on twenty-five percent of the gross door receipts.

A reviewer for *The Magic Circular*, witnessing the performance at the Brighton Hippodrome, gives full descriptions of the "Vril" and "Ayesha" illusions:

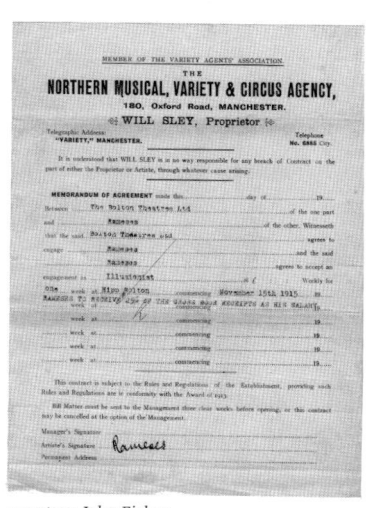

courtesy John Fisher

> The 'tabs' are now lowered, and attendants place in front of them a flat platform about 6x 3ft x 2in. thick, and raised some 5in. from the stage, on four legs. To one end of this platform are attached several stout coils of electric wire. On one side of the stage is placed a table supporting certain low lamps, switches, and a powerful induction coil.

Two attendants carry on 'Vril,' a full-sized Pierrot figure, which is stood on the raised platform. Connection is made by means of a length of flexible 'lead' and a plug, between one arm of the figure and the electrical apparatus, which starts 'buzzing,' and the figure goes through a series of jerky movements, its eyes lighting up at intervals. After shuffling to one end of the raised platform, it bends backwards until the back of its head is on the same level as its feet. When sitting on a chair, a small square board is placed on its knees, the chair is pulled away; and the figure remains 'sitting on nothing' with the whole body inclined well behind the feet.

Rameses stands on the small board on the figure's knees, places one foot on its chest, and presses the body down until it is lying back in a line with the knees. Finally, the figure rises erect (after Rameses has returned to switches), and is carried off by attendants. This item, though on similar lines to other 'mechanical' figures in many respects, is well ahead of them, and the latter part clearly left the audience guessing.

The final effect, entitled 'Ayesha,' which is presented on the full stage, is one of the must puzzling that has been seen for some time, and provides even the 'initiated' with considerable food for thought. After standing erect on the stage, the lady assistant rises into the air, and assumes a number of graceful poses, floating from side to side of the stage rising and falling in rhythmic movements, bending backwards, and executing a 'dance in the air.'

During all these movements, Rameses passes beneath and around her. After rising again to a height of about six feet, she 'skips' in the air, with a piece of thick bent cane (this should puzzle some of the 'wise ones!' A very, effective serpentine skirt dance is performed in the air after the necessary dress as been donned, and the lady finally alights on the stage, and runs down to the footlights.

To conclude, a sheet is draped over her, she rises straight up into the air, and a small solid hoop is dropped over her from the head downwards, several times; the cloth is then jerked away, and 'Ayesha' has vanished. . . .

At times, while in the air, the girl turns completely round in an easy natural manner, showing her back and sides, and that whole thing is performed in a smooth, fairly rapid manner, which is very pleasing, and provides a valuable lesson to those performers who still present the old levitation from couch, and slow passing; of hoop, with which the public is now so familiar.[31]

In January of 1917 Albert even found the time to visit Liverpool Street Station to say au revoir to Chung Ling Soo prior to his world tour. There was a great camaraderie amongst the pros even then.

A particularly spirited review of Rameses' performance at the Holborn Empire Theatre, in October, compares the Rameses show with other "oriental" themed acts:

> Rameses had it his own way at The Holborn Music Hall where he 'out Egypts Egypt' in the spectacularly Oriental act which he has made famous in every London and provincial hall.
>
> There are some Oriental acts which are so 'dusky' that a good wash and spring clean seems to be the only 'magic' suitable to relieve them from the dust of the past ages — and bookings!
>
> Rameses must, however, be sufficiently modern to employ a vacuum cleaner for that 'dinginess' of which we have hinted has no pace in his act, which is bright, clean and polished in every sense of the word.[32]

Rameses' well-polished Egyptian spectacle had earned him international acclaim, huge American audiences, and Royal attention in London. His victory in the UK, at the largest Hippodrome theatres, was undeniable, and fellow magicians sang his praises. Riding this wave of success, Marchinski decided to become a producer. ❋

CHAPTER THREE

❧ BEYOND MAGIC

THE PERFORMER is responsible for the statement that:

> Rameses is about to blossom out as a proprietor and manager. He is said to have acquired the Empire Theatre, the oldest place of amusement in Southend. If this is true, the sea-siders may expect to see some magic.[1]

In August of 1917 (as mentioned earlier) Rameses took a lease on the New Empire Theatre Southend. Goldston had this to say:

> RAMESES, the Oriental magician, will in future be seen in a new role, and for a magician, an unusual one. He is opening the Empire, Southend-on-Sea, with the controversial and much discussed play, 'Damaged Goods,' on Monday, August 6th.[2]

Even with contracts signed, Albert was still on the road. In August and September of 1917 he was at Kingston Empire.

Still performing, Rameses & Company appeared at the Grand Complimentary Benefit at the Empire Theatre on April 8th 1918.

Within a seemingly short space of time Marchinski's new role as producer would attract a different kind of attention from the press.

Reporting on legal proceedings surrounding Marchinski's lease on the Southend Theatre, *The Southend Telegraph* says:

Southend Empire Theatre

In the Chancery Division of the High Court, on Friday, before Mr Justice Sargant, Mr Jenkins, K.C. mentioned the case of Leigh v. Rameses, in which the plaintiff asked for an injunction to restrain the defendant for interfering with his use or occupation of the Empire Theatre, Southend. Mr Jenkins said last week Mrs Rameses was the plaintiff's representative and defendants were persons to whom she purported to have let the theatre.

Today, however, the proceedings would be abortive because the superior landlord had interfered and claimed to put an end to the lease, in which all the parties claimed an interest on the ground of alleged bankruptcy of the general lessee. The only thing now to do was to ask his lordship to let the motion again stand over for a week in order that the plaintiff might consider her position.[3]

By the end of the year The Empire Theatre was under the new management of Mr. Austin Fryer (whose real name was William Edward de Clery). In 1906 Fryer had taken over the deserted Hengler's Circus on Argyll Street London. (The Fryer/ Hengler's lease was taken over by the London Palladium.) For three and half years though he ran it with so much success that he was able to spend £10,000 on its redecoration. With his vast experience Fryer brought all manner of new events mostly opera to the Southend venue, including: The Royal Carl Rosa Opera Company presenting *The Tales of Hoffmann, Cavalleria Rustic Ana, Pagliacci, Carmen*, and *Madame Butterfly*. It

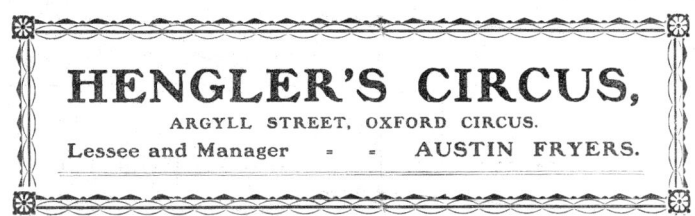

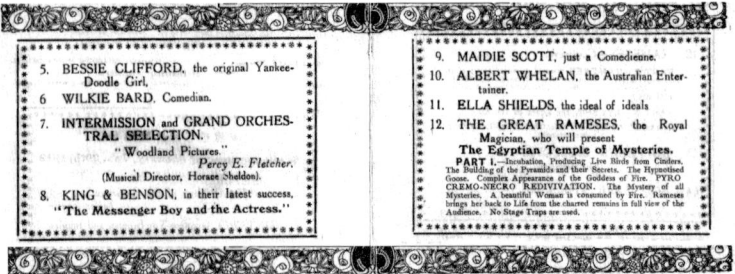

was ironic that Rameses was playing at The Palladium for two weeks at this very same time.

From Fryer the lease was taken over by the London Palladium. Ironically Rameses was playing at The Palladium for two weeks at this very same time.

Fryer then became Albert's sole business representative and manager (to whom all communications would be addressed) and sent out this press release:

> 'The Great Rameses' The Royal Magician is the latest 'star' recruit for the cinema. He will appear in strong character parts, and has an extensive repertoire in Yiddish plays in which he will probably repeat some of his earlier stage successes, for although it is not generally known, he had achieved no inconsiderable position as an actor before he had decided to become a 'star' Music Hall turn as, an Illusionist. His first appearance was under the management of Mr. John Lawson in a sketch called 'The Shield of David'. Mr. Lawson's choice for the part lay between the late Mr. Leonard Boyne and Rameses, and the latter was naturally, elated when the preference was given to him: He appeared under the Melville management at the Adelphi and other theatres, and on one occasion owing to three actors falling under the fell influence of 'Flu;' he took at a moments notice, no fewer than seven parts in one play.
>
> In Africa he was a member of Mr. William Haviland's well know Shakespearean Company playing a variety of parts, including 'Neckludorf' in 'Resurrection.' He afterwards became a member of Mr. Leonard Rayne's Stock` Company, a fellow member being – Mr. Godfrey Tearle, and made an extensive tour, of the principal African towns. He then ran a Yiddish Season under his own management producing in Capetown and Johannesburg

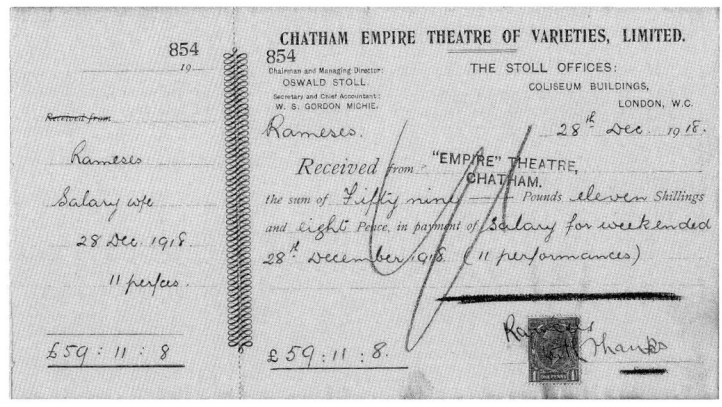

no fewer than 300 famous Yiddish and other plays. This season was by arrangement with Mr. Frank Wheeler and the late Mr. T.B.Young of Messrs Macdonald and Young.

His position as an actor of strong character parts was becoming well established when Mr L Sacks suggested to him the idea of starting as an illusionist, and as the late Mr. Tom Barrasford backed up the suggestion by offering him the use of the Britannia Theatre for six weeks free of charge for rehearsals he accepted the friendly advice and assistance with the result that is well known . . .

There is no doubt that Rameses would have attained a leading position as an actor of strong character parts had he remained on the regular stage and his great talents and histrionic experience will undoubtedly stand him in such good stead on the screen that his success is assured.

But legal troubles would continue. *The Southend Telegraph*:

MRS RAMESES ACTION FOR POSSESSION

The case of Rameses v. Ryde came on for hearing on Tuesday before Mr. Justice Astbury in the Chancery Division and was another step in the litigation over the Southend Empire Theatre. The plaintiff Mrs Rose Rameses sought a declaration that she was a tenant and entitled to possession of the Empire Theatre...and she asked for possession of the theatre and refreshment rooms and cloak rooms, and an injunction to restrain the defendants, the Southend-on-Sea Theatre Company, from excluding

> THE GREATEST SENSATION OF THE AGE.
> **Absolutely Original.**
> The only Magical Act of its kind in the World.
>
> ## "RAMESES"
> *The Egyptian Wonder Worker.*
>
> ## "Egyptian Temple of Mysteries"
> ORIGINAL.   NOVEL.   SENSATIONAL.
> Astounding, startling, and inexplicable Illusions ever seen in England.
>
> MOST ELABORATE SCENERY AND COSTUMES EVER SEEN.
>
> See the Greatest Spectacle of Stage Setting.
> See the appearance of the **"Master Magician."**
> See the Mysterious Light.
> See the Incubation.
> See the **Creation of the Fire Goddess.**
> See **Her Destruction by Fire.**
> See the Redi-vivation in mid-air.
> See the Greatest Astounding Sensation
>
> PYRO-CREMO-NECRO-REDI VIVATION
>
> **This Week — MIDDLESEX.**
>
> All Communications direct to—
>
> ## "RAMESES."

her from the occupation, and she asked for damages and payment of a certain specific sum; in the alternative there was a claim against the Receiver, Mr Nerney, who plaintiff said, granted a lease to another party which she contended he had no power to grant.

...Mr Nerney was appointed receiver and manager and there was a foreclosure action in 1919. The receiver granted a lease of the theatre to Albert Rameses, the husband of the plaintiff, and he becoming bankrupt the lease came to an end and subsequently the receiver suggested that his wife should take the lease of the theatre which she agreed to do. One day when the theatre was open, Mr Randal, a clerk in the employment of a firm of solicitors, came down and Mrs Rameses being away at the time, he locked the door and she had not been able to get in again. The receiver had let another tenant for a short period and the question was whether he had power to do so. Counsel argued that he had not and had not finished his argument when the hearing stood adjourned.

The hearing was resumed on Wednesday and eventually the case was settled; the defendant, Mr Ryde, undertaking to pay within fourteen days £355, and the plaintiff's costs to be taxed or agreed, and the Receiver's costs to be his costs in the receivership. On theses terms the proceedings were stayed.[4]

Despite his new artistic and professional endeavours, Albert continued touring with his illusion show. In the next year he performed at the Manchester Hippodrome, The Middlesex, The Leicester Palace Theatre, The Coliseum, and The Chatham Empire Theatre Of Varieties.

In the April 1920 issue of *The Sphinx* Max Holden confirmed Marchinski's continued success and hinted at the possibility of another American tour:

> Rameses, the Egyptian Illusionist, is headlining on all the Stoll Theatres. I recently had the pleasure of being on the same bill with Rameses, and what a wonderful Magician and Showman; American Magicians will remember Rameses as having played the Orpheum Circuit in America a few years back, and there is a possibility that he may be again seen in America in the near future.[5]

Albert proved beyond doubt that he was a better performer than he was a Producer Manager. A lot of potentially successful artists need good management. He may well have been badly advised, or someone could have seen in him an easy target for this financial venture. One will never know. ✻

Three-sheet lithograph, David Allen & Sons. Courtesy of Mike Caveney.

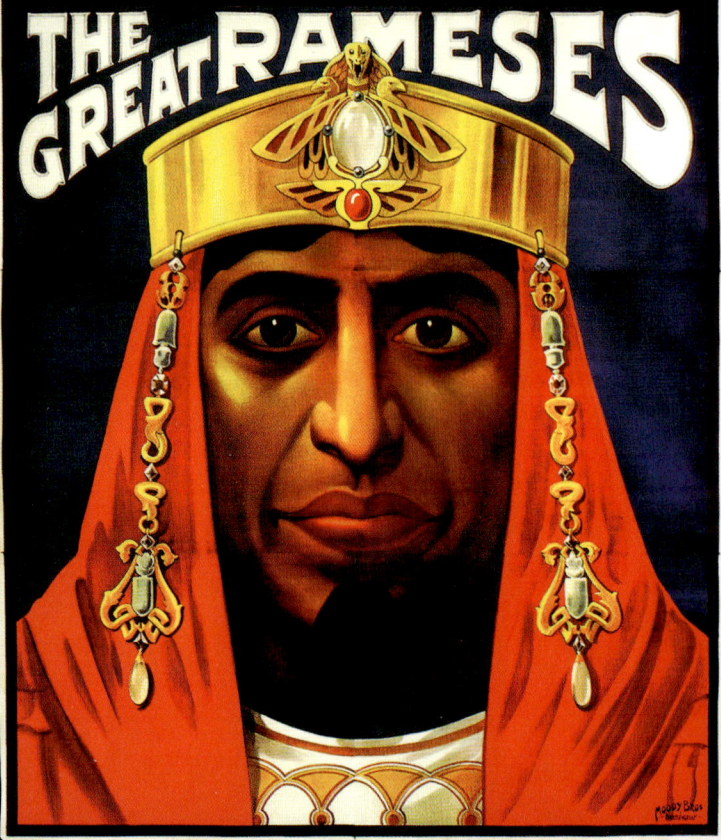

Eight-sheet billboard lithograph, Moody Bros. Courtesy of Mario Carrandi.

Half-sheet "butterfly" lithograph, David Allen & Sons. Courtesy of Dr. Timothy Moore.

Telephone: 885 PADDINGTON.

WHEATLAND & SONS
THE BEST AND CHEAPEST
HOUSE FURNISHERS.
CASH or DEFERRED PAYMENTS
101, HIGH ROAD, KILBURN.

KILBURN EMPIRE.
TELEPHONE: PADDINGTON 698.

Managing Director ... ... CHARLES GULLIVER
Manager ... ... DAVID JAMES, Jnr.   Licensee ... ... FRANCIS J. PEPPER
Acting Manager ... ... P. ST. CROIX   Stage Manager ... ... W. HOOKE
Musical Director ... ... ARTHUR FELLOWES

MONDAY, FEB. 15th, 1915.   **TWICE NIGHTLY at 6.20 & 8.45**

Before and during Overture Interesting Slide Advertisements will be shown. For particulars, apply to Advertising Department, London Theatres of Varieties, Holborn Restaurant, W.C.

Ladies are respectfully requested to remove their Hats so as to afford greater comfort to persons seated behind.

1. **OVERTURE**
2. **BILLY FRENCH**, Light Comedian and Dancer
3. **TERRY TWINS**, Boxing Comedians
4. **CELIA STORM & CO.**, in
   ### "ALIAS IRISH TESSIE"
   An American Detective Sketch
   Bill Keegan, a Central Office Detective, or "Bull" ... Mr. RICHARD NORTON
   Kathleen, Tessie's Maid from the old Country ... Miss ADA D. HATCHWELL
   Tessie O'Brien, alias "Irish Tessie," a Notorious Shoplifter ... Miss CELIA STORM
   SCENE ... ... Tessie O'Brien's Apartments in 45 Street, N.Y.
5. **THE McNAUGHTONS**, (FRED & GUS) In Fresh Outbursts of Brotherly Love
6. **SAMMY SHIELDS**, The Football Enthusiast
7. **VICTORIA MONKS**, John Bull's Girl, in her Latest Successes
8. **FIVE X-RAYS**, presented by JOSH CLIFTON. Mad Athletes
9. **CHRISTIE DUO** Comedy Dancing Eccentrics
10. **THE MEYMOTTS**, presented by J. F. ELLISTON
    Supported by Miss IRENE GRAHAM, in the New Comedy Playlet, by HARRY EDLIN, entitled **"IN THE FUTURE"**
11. **FOUR WARDS**, In Harmony, Comedy and Dance
12. **RAMESES**. The Royal Magician, who will present
    ### THE EGYPTIAN TEMPLE OF MYSTERIES
    PART 1.
    Incubation. Producing Live Birds from Cinders. The Building of the Pyramids and their Secrets. The Hypnotised Goose. The Complex Appearance of the Goddess of Fire. PYRO-CREMO-NECRO REDIVIVATION. The Mystery of all Mysteries. A beautiful Woman consumed by Fire, Rameses brings her back to Life from the charred remains, in full view of the Audience. No Stage Traps are used.
    PART 2.
    RAMESES Presents the Great Query of the Universe
    ### "VRIL"
    The Acme of the Uncanny. Is "VRIL," human? mechanical? or a being under the abysmal powers of RAMESES.
    PART 3.
    ### "AYESHA," the Sensation of the Age.
    REMARKABLE ! MYSTERIOUS ! SCIENTIFIC ! WEIRDLY EXCITING ! SENSATIONAL !

PRICES OF ADMISSION ARE: Boxes (to seat 4 persons) 10/6 and 7/6. Extra Seats 2/6 & 2/-; Fauteuils 1/6, bookable in advance 2d. extra ; Circle 1/-, bookable in advance 2d. extra ; Pit 8d. ; Gallery (Upholstered Seating) 3d. Saturdays (2nd House only) Bank Holidays and Special Occasions ; Fauteuils 1/9 ; Circle 1/3 ; Pit 8d.; Gallery 4d. Seats may be booked by Post, Telephone or Wire. 'Phone No. : Paddington 698.

Box Office open from 10 a.m. till 10 p.m. Furniture supplied by A. Simmons & Co., Complete House Furnishers, 81 & 83, Lanesfield Street, Kilburn Lane, N.W. Floral Decorations by G. W. Finch, High Road, Kilburn.

In accordance with the Requirements of the London County Council:—
(a) The public may leave at the end of the performance by all exit and entrance doors, and such doors must at that time be open. (b) All gangways, passages and staircases must be kept entirely free from chairs or any other obstruction. (c) Persons must not be permitted to stand or sit in any of the intersecting gangways (and if standing be permitted in the gangways at the sides and rear of the seating sufficient space must be left for persons to pass easily to and fro. (d) The Safety Curtain must be lowered about the middle of the performance so as to ensure it being in proper working order.

FOR THE BEST DENTISTRY OBTAINABLE CONSULT
Mr. H. C. BRAUN, R.D.S.,
Surgeon-Dentist, 1, Kilburn Square, High Rd., N.W.
Established over 20 years. (Facing the Gas Company)
'PHONE: 3985 Paddington.

High Grade Artificial Teeth at Lowest Possible Cash Fees. Satisfaction Guaranteed. Expert in Gold Crowns and Bridge Work. The Most Up-to-Date Equipped Surgery in the District

ANALGESIA   The last word in Painless Treatment. Huge Success in America
NO PAIN. NO UNCONSCIOUSNESS.

Rameses headlines a 12-act bill at the Kilburn Empire. Courtesy of Mike Caveney.

Rameses postcards. Courtesy of Paul Kieve.

Rameses playing cards. Author's collection.

Rameses and Ayesha. Courtesy of John Fisher.

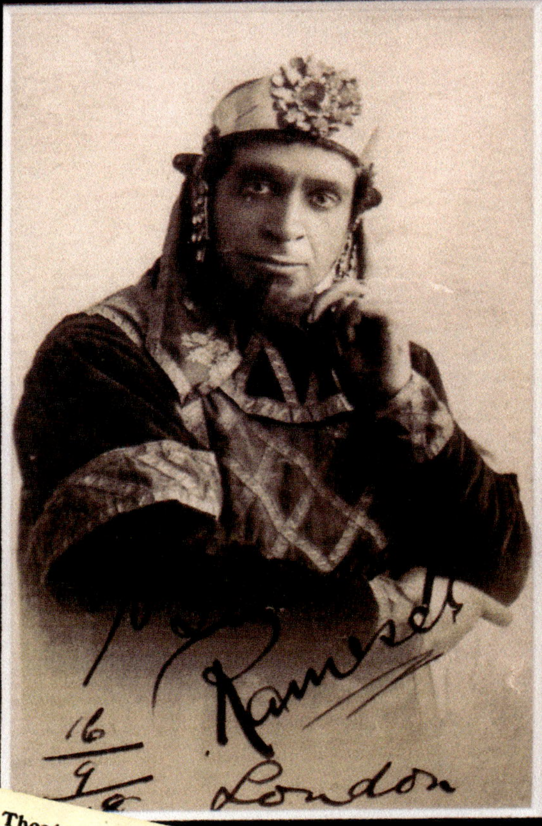

EMPIRE Theatre, Southend-on-Sea. 760
Licensee ALBERT RAMESES.
Grand Complimentary Benefit Week
Under Distinguished Patronage
Monday, April 8th, 1918
And 5 following Nights.
Matinees Wednesday and Saturday at 2.30.
The Great Rameses,
Supported by a Full London Star Co.
Fauteuils 2/- Tax 4d.
RAMESES
This Voucher is available for any ONE Performance during the week, and should be taken to the Box Office and exchanged for a Numbered and Reserved Seat

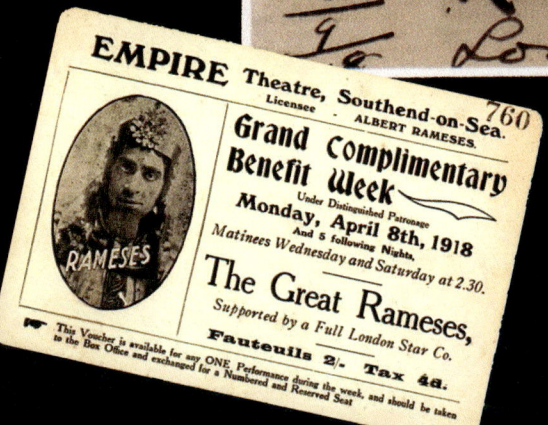

Photograph and ticket. Courtesy of Andy Lansing

Half-sheet lithograph, David Allen & Sons. Courtesy of Norm Nielsen.

CHAPTER FOUR

EGYPT BECKONS AT LAST

WHILE MARCHINSKI'S FINANCIAL PROBLEMS were beginning to peak, he was still playing to packed houses and seeking out creative inspiration. During the summer of 1920 – instead of touring the US – Albert and Rosie travelled to Egypt, searching for new ideas and venues. They left London on July 30th 1920 on the P & O S.S. Kaiser-I-Hind and sailed, via Marseilles to Port Said.

Following their visit, an article appeared in the Christmas 1920 edition of *The Performer*:

MEETING MY ANCESTORS by Rameses

In common with most Magicians I have frequently been asked my opinion of spiritualism – a subject much in the public eye – it should be mouth shouldn't it? – these days. A topic, too, upon which, controversy has at times overstepped the limits of polite debate and become somewhat heated.

Now I am not going to enter the arena with some new thought or suggestion as to the occult or the spirit world. No dry as dust dissertation shall come from my pen, for is this not the Christmas Season, and are we not all wishful of presenting as joyous an aspect as possible? This, apart altogether from the question as to whether I am able to cast any fresh light upon a much debated matter or not.

Why mention spiritualism at all then you ask? Well, I was to-day reminded of an incident which occurred a few months ago while I was performing in Alexandria. It was a chance meeting in Oxford Street with an old Egyptian acquaintance which brought the incident to my mind. Talking over things in general and Egypt in particular, my friend referred to the incident which I now propose to relate.

I was playing Alexandria at the time and one evening as we were all sitting in the hotel lounge, conversation turned upon 'fakirs' and from thence to 'spiritualism.' The company present was almost fifty- fifty 'pro' and 'anti,' and so, naturally, the discussion was brisk, but, equally naturally, somewhat inconclusive. Then they appealed to me, for my profession was known and who, more likely to have delved into such subject as a magician?

I disclaimed any special knowledge and refused to assent to the proposition that I should decide so debatable a point as to whether spiritualism, was or was not genuine. Indeed, I said, I had given but little thought to the subject – but I thought there might be something in it – or there might not. From my own observation, however, I was convinced of one thing, and that was that there was nothing accomplished by a professional medium which any self respecting magicians could not do. At which the sceptics in the crowd laughed and the believers fastened on me forsaking all other controversial opponents, and one, who had been most vigorous in his denunciation of all unbelievers, issued a challenge. If I would but go to a séance with him he would guarantee that I should there receive sufficient evidence to convert me into a confirmed spiritualist. His words were backed up by a friend whose accent denoted a more than passing acquaintance with New York.

A appointment was made, and that evening in a house a little off the main street I met my friend the challenger with a dozen other people, to whom I was introduced, but as is usual in such cases, whose names I scarcely caught, and do not remember. The majority were members of some psychical society or other – the rest a few honest doubters or open-minded inquirers. My mental attitude I will not state.

The room we were ushered into was rectangular and longer than it was broad by a good many feet. At one end where there was no window a curtain hung across the room, so shutting off a square space, three sides of which were blank wall and the fourth the heavy hanging curtain. In a chair in the centre of this square sat the medium -a lady, securely tied with silk strands, the knots in which are most difficult to untie in light and practically impossible to untie in the dark. In addition a steel chain was padlocked around the medium's waist and to the chair

To me it seemed obvious that the medium could not move from her seat-while absence of windows and doors ensured that no one could enter the square except by passing through we others who sat in a semicircle facing the curtain — that is, sat in chairs the larger portion of the room.

As I entered, I noticed that there were men-servants at the two doors which opened into the room, and the keys were turned in the locks when we were all in and the bolts were shot.

Lights were put out with the exception of a small ruby lamp, which gave just sufficient light to show one the neighbouring sitter but no more.

Silence for what appeared many minutes but what may have been only a few seconds, ensued and immediately mysterious noises and tappings and movements were heard. Then a 'voice' asked if any specific manifestation was required, and I in my pride I thought of my forerunner-he who bore the name I am known by-the great Rameses II.

A perceptible lightening of the impenetrable darkness which marked the spot where the curtain shut off the medium from the observers, and a slight tremor of the hangings; then a strong light which assumed form, faint at first but gathering strength, until at last, in front of us stood Rameses himself in ancient robes.

Recovering from my surprise, I found my voice and questioned the long-dead but veritably present potentate. Intelligible answer I could not get — but that I put down to my ignorance of the language used. Then, with an assumption of boldness which ill coincided with my inward trepidation, I put the matter to a test. Quickly and surreptitiously, I thrust a pin deep into the leg of the apparition — 'Say. Bo, I'm not a gol-darned pin-cushion,' was the prefatory exercise to a string of imprecations. Then I knew!

This visit to Alexandria, Cairo and Port Said was borne out by an article written in 1951 by Victor Farelli. In *The Pentagram* he said:

> As a matter of fact, I stopped in the same hotel with him, for over a month, in Cairo, Egypt in 1920. And I met him here in London on more than one occasion. Horace Goldin, who was in Cairo shortly before my arrival there, packed the theatre night after night with Australian and other troops, and some years later Rameses appeared. He did indifferent business in Cairo, but his success in Alexandria with the Ayesha Floating Lady can only be described as phenomenal. I have it on the best of authority that the people who engaged him made £1,000 in one month with the show![1]

Magician Tom Melbourne's son, then about fourteen years of age, accompanied his father to Egypt and got a job as a temporary assistant to Rameses. One day he said to his father: "Daddy, there is a matinee to-day! We will be on the stage TWICE! Isn't it GLORIOUS?"

Albert and Rosie were back home in time for the winter season and in November they were at the Empire Theatre, Chatham. In December he would perform at the Wood Green Empire and the Bristol Hippodrome. In *The Performer* all the artists took adverts offering their Christmas greetings to one and all. Albert Marchinski placed a full-page advert and it was noted that he was living by this time at 1 Essex Terrace Southend-on-Sea.

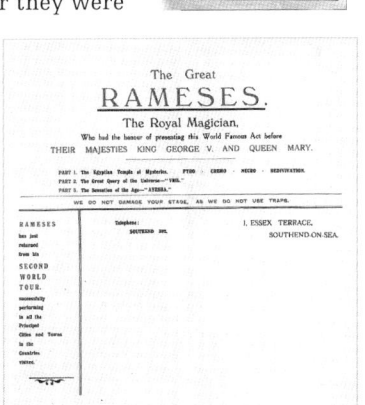

courtesy Southend Museum

Despite his travels in Egypt and continued success as a performer, Marchinski's financial ruin would soon become public. *The Gazette* stated:

RAMESES, Albert, lately carrying on business at, or residing at, The Empire Theatre, Alexandra Street, Southend-on-Sea, Essex. THEATRICAL MANAGER and ARTIST.

Court – CHELMSFORD.
No. of Matter – 8 of 1918.
Date of Order – April 19, 1920 (Order varying Order-made on Oct. 14, 1918).
Nature of Order made – Order of Discharge granted on Oct. 14, 1918, varied, and in lieu thereof Bankrupt discharged subject to consenting to Judgment being entered against him by the Trustee for £150, and £1 10s. costs of Judgment.
(Note. – £150 paid in lieu of entering up Judgment.) [2]

This did not, however, put an end to his prestigious performances. He was back again at The London Coliseum on January 24th 1921.

By 1922 Albert Rameses was living at 171 Queen Road London W2.

On March 5th 1923 Rameses appeared for the week at The Alhambra Theatre situated in Leicester Square London with a capacity around 3,000.

In September and October of 1923 he would give nightly performances at St. George's Hall (that had a smaller capacity of 550 seats). *The Magician Monthly* reports that, "The patrons of St. George's Hall cannot complain of any lack of variety in the programmes. Rameses played a very successful month at the Hall." [3]

On December 21st 1923, Charles Gulliver (who was the Managing Director of the London Theatre of Varieties, a company that controlled dozens of theatres in the country and others within the London area) played Father Christmas to over 10,000 children in and around London by holding a giant children's party in one of his theatres: the Olympia Theatre Shoreditch. Rameses suitably decorated

courtesy Paul Kieve

the theatre with all the usual festive trimmings, while on stage the show included some special Christmas "magic." This was repeated a week later at the Islington Empire.

A January 1924 article in *The Magician Monthly* briefly mentions Rameses' presence at Maskelyne's, "At the time of writing Rameses is playing a return engagement at Maskelyne's, his principle item being the favorite one contributed by 'Ayesha, Queen of the Air.' " [4]

THE GULLIVER CIRCUIT

Appertaining to this particular presentation the editor John Young in *The Magic Circular* remembers:

> We well remember seeing Rameses' illusion act at Maskelyne's, but the only item that stands out vividly is his production of girl assistants from a cabinet which had the appearance of an Egyptian tomb, i.e. the doorway was narrower at the top than at the bottom, hence the internal dimensions of the cabinet were greater each side of the door towards the top which materially assisted with the concealment of the occupants. [5]

In February and March of 1924, Rameses would appear again at St. George's Hall alongside P.T. Selbit presenting "The Man without a Middle" and comedy juggler Eddie Gray.

At this time Rameses was still making new additions to his time-tested repertoire of illusions. According to *The Magician Monthly*, in 1929:

> Rameses was performing with great success at the Pierhill Pavilion Southend. Still billed as The Royal Magician it was reported that his wine and water trick brought him great applause. [6]

In an issue of *The Magic Wand* for 1928, Rameses provides professional details on the age-old "Wine and Water" trick, as well as his own thoughts on the performance of magic:

WINE AND WATER

'What, again,' I can hear readers say when they see this heading. Read on. Although old, I venture to suggest that there is no experiment with liquids which can surpass the old wine and water effect, moreover, in this particular version there is only one tumbler used, and further, both jug and tumbler are free from any mechanical contrivances and may be examined if necessary.

That's better; now I can see you slip farther into your 'Berkeley,' puffing hard at the old pipe, while you have taken a better grip on the Wand.

Effect. Performer introduces a jug of water, which he holds in left hand, and an ordinary plain glass in the right. He drinks some of the water then spins or throws the tumbler into the air. Catching the glass he fills it from jug when the water in the tumbler is found to have changed to wine. The wine is now poured back into jug. Result, all wine. Now without any false moves, the wine is poured from the jug and the tumbler is seen to contain clear water, which on being poured back results in a jug full of water as at first.

Requirements. Jug and tumbler silicylate of soda, tincture of iron (steel drops), oxalic acid and an empty two-penny 'Fairy' dye tube. Into the jug is placed a pinch of silicylate of soda, and in the tumbler four or five drops of tincture of iron, The dye-tube is half-filled with saturated solution of oxalic acid.

St. George's Hall, Langham Place W.I.

The jug and tumbler are on table, and the dye tube is behind them. In commencing, the performer places the phial in the ball of the left thumb, the tip of the thumb covering the opening. The jug is taken in the left hand, the free fingers grasping the handle, while the right hand picks up the tumbler. A little of the water may be tasted.

Now water is poured into the tumbler where it apparently changes to wine. This also may be tasted (silicylate, and steel drops will do you good, so do not be afraid of the taste.) The contents of tumbler are emptied into the jug, giving, apparently a jug full of wine, then comes the crucial move. The tumbler is brought over the top of the jug and rattled against it, and at the same time the tip of the thumb is removed from the tube, allowing the oxalic to run into tumbler. As this takes a fraction of a second, and as in rattling the jug the performer is apparently only emphasizing the fact that both jug and tumbler are free from preparation, no one dreams that anything has been accomplished.

It only remains to pour some wine into the tumbler and then back into the jug to bring this pretty effect to a conclusion.

Suggestions: For the benefit of those who have never worked the wine and water effect in any of its forms, I think the following data will be useful. Three pennyworth of oxalic acid emptied into an ordinary pickle jar filled with water, makes the required saturated solution: – In the case of the amateur and semi-professional this is sufficient to last nearly a year. Twopennyworth of Silicylate of Soda will last equally as long, provided that one uses only 'enough to cover a sixpence,' for each performances. Three pennyworth of tincture of iron completes the stock of chemicals.

The foregoing I think, give the most satisfactory results. They are safe to take (except the oxalic acid, of course), and further, the 'wine' is a rich ruby red. Always keep the steel drops tightly corked as it has a devastating effect on silks. Always carry two or three dye tubes as they are very fragile. It is best to keep them in the cardboard cylinders in which they are sold.

The above effect should be worked fairly quickly, nowadays, the old-fashioned talk, and very little mystery is of no use. Effects should be presented quickly, and although the conjurer must talk, he must be doing something at the same time. A whole string of gags such as, "Although this is a tumbler, it does not perform any acrobatic feats," prolongs the experiment unnecessarily. Besides which, the conjurer is paid for his magical abilities primarily, not for his efforts as a comedian. Perhaps the following patter will give a little idea of what the Americans so aptly define as 'snap'.

Patter. 'This next little effect was evolved in America to elude the prohibition agents: Should one require a drink of water' (drink here) 'This is it sometimes used for diluting whisky, on the other hand' (spin tumbler while talking) 'should you desire something stronger, well here it is:' (Look at the audience, turn left side on, smile broadly and take a good drink of wine and don't forget to look as if you are enjoying it). 'Should some friends call, well pour it back (suiting actions to words) and here we have all wine... I like doing this because I can put lots of spirit into it.' (As this is said, you rattle jug With tumbler and the deed is done:) 'Should the prohibition authorities call, and ask you, what you are doing with wine, you say Not wine, sir, but ordinary water, (pour wine into' tumbler, which results in water). And what about the jug? (Pour water back into jug). Why sir, ordinary water.'

It is unnecessary to add that the above patter is not suited for everyone's style of showing, but I think it will give some idea of the speed at which it should be worked.[7]

Verrall Wass detailed this improvement in his book *Astound Your Audience* along with other items that were not part of the stage show:

RAMESES' WINE AND WATER

I saw Rameses perform this trick at the Pier Hill Pavilion, Southend-on-Sea, some months before his death, not in 1896 as Will Goldston erroneously stated. Here I should like to record that this is the only occasion on which I have found an error of fact in a Goldston book.

Rameses made the old wine and water trick seem entirely new to the audience, it was a stroke of near-genius; near genius adapts, genius creates. There are many reminiscences of Rameses' last days I could relate, telling of his entertainments at the Kursaal, Southend, his operation and death, but I am saving these for a future book.

The small hall was well filled for the special evening of the Beatrice Gomez concert party, and Rameses, who was billed for the one night only, was undoubtedly the hit of the evening, although he only performed three items: the four-ace trick with giant cards, his version of the wine and water trick, and the passing of two ropes through three men of whom I was one. But to the wine and water trick. It was the 'Osoeasy' non-poisonous chemicals version he used: sodium salicylate dissolved in the clear water, phenolphthalein solution for turning the supposed unprepared water red, and a few drops of tartaric acid dissolved in water for turning the "red wine" back to water. On the table he had a carafe of wine (sodium carbonate and phenolphthalein solution in water) and a syphon of soda-water (sodium salicylate in water). In front of these stood two tumblers; one with a little phenolphthalein solution, the other with a few drops of tartaric acid in water. On the same table were three small sheets of paper. Two members of the audience, a lady and a gentleman, were invited on the stage. Rameses gave each of them a piece of paper, taking the third himself. He instructed them in the art of making a paper cone with such a confusion of movements that although the gentleman succeeded comparatively easily, the lady made several laughter-provoking attempts, and finally had to accept the cone Rameses had twisted up.

Into each of these cones, held above eye-level, he dropped one of the tumblers. He squirted pseudo-soda-water into one tumbler, screwed up the mouth of the cone, and poured wine into the other tumbler, afterwards screwing up the other cone. With true magical artistry he announced, 'I will make the tumblers change places,' rather than say, 'I will make the wine and water change places.' When the cones were undone, and the tumblers revealed, it was seen how well he had succeeded.[8]

This highlights his ability for taking something we have all dismissed as perhaps too simple and trivial and turning it into a major stage effect.

It was a masterstroke, and in short, showmanship incarnate. Whatever business failures Marchinkski experienced, his abilities as an inventive and charismatic magician were continually growing. ❋

… CHAPTER FIVE

THE PALACE OF ILLUSIONS

LESS THAN A MILE from the old Empire Theatre was a venue that brought back unhappy memories for Marchinski, the Kursaal. This was virtually on the seafront and had various attractions within one fascinating complex. It was a bit of a step down for poor Marchinski, but it was work and he needed to eat and support his wife.

The Southend Kursaal Company building was completed in 1901, with a great silver dome over the entrance. The word "Kursaal" is

German, meaning a "Cure Hall" or spa, and it seems to have been adapted to mean a place of healthy amusement.

The Southend Kursaal was the world's first theme park, pre-dating Coney Island in America. Designed by Campbell Sherri, the main build-

ing and its dome were at the cutting edge of architecture.

The Kursaal included a circus, a ballroom and an arcade complemented by other sideshows and amusements. Each one would be competing for the same customers. There was also a skating rink, a dining hall and a billiard room. There were many "firsts" at the Kursaal. The world's first "Lady Lion Tamer" and the world's first female "Wall of Death" rider performed here; it was the first venue in England to display Al Capone's personal car from Chicago, not to mention Eric the sixty ton stuffed whale.

The outside talkers had to attract the crowds that entered the center walkway. By keeping to the middle there was less chance of people being "caught." The "spielers" were up to all sorts of antics and you could hear them beckoning potential customers. "Did you get one?" "Did they give you one when you came in?" "Did they Shwype the Kypes?" This gibberish would  inevitably attract one or two people. These "barkers" hoped that others would follow so they could really sell what they had to offer.

The catch phrases "By the Dome it's Known" and "One Bright Spot" were recognized around the country as the Kursaal became famous for its shows, attractions, and amusements.

Thankfully, the building still stands today. Regrettably, though, there is little left of the original, other than the trademark dome and façade. Sadly, it has bowed to commercial pressures, and is now a bowling alley.

Southend was the nearest seaside resort to London; it is approximately forty-five miles east of the city. It was always, and still is, thought of as "London by the Sea." When Liberal MP Sir John Lubbock's Bank Holiday Act of 1871 came into force, the first Monday in August became a national holiday, and all over the city the London, Tilbury, and Southend Railway Companies posted bills advertising Southend as the capital's nearest seaside resort. Many would travel by train or, for the more affluent, motorcar each weekend to enjoy the local attractions, as well the beach. Southend boasted the longest pier in the world at three-point-one miles! This Victorian construction had its own single gauge tramway to take patrons from one end to the other.

In 1928 a young George Mackenzie – who later opened his Scottish magic emporium and produced *Mac's Mysteries* magic magazine – worked for Rameses at The Kursaal.

With many sideshows and attractions, The Kursaal, Southend was a fascinating place for a family to visit. There was, however, much competition for the Rameses *Temple of Magic and Palace of Illusion* shows.

In 1929 "The Wall of Death" – the daredevil motor cycling ride – was introduced. Other side-show attractions included: "The Electric Chair," "Togo the Snake Handler," and "The Snake Pit." There was also "The Midget Mansion" with Colonel and Mrs. Cox "themselves midgets without deformity of any kind." One big attraction was

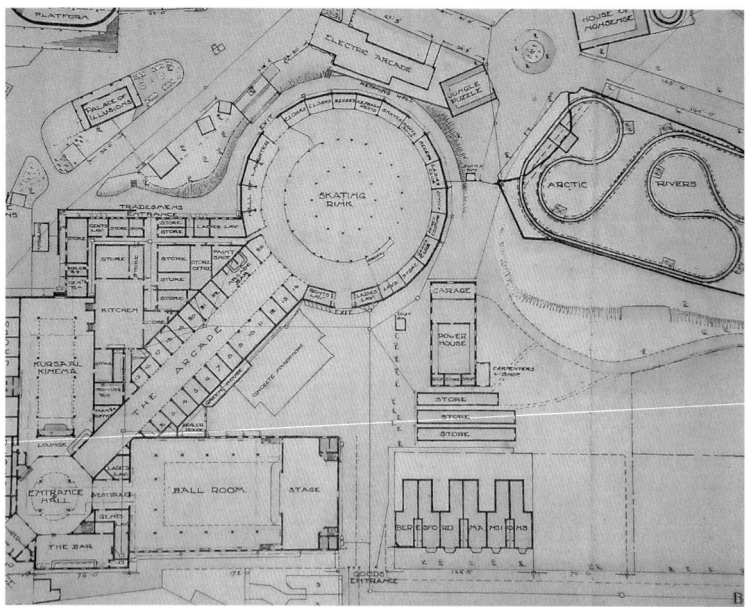

courtesy Southend Museum

Rameses	Egyptian Wonder Worker. Touring the World in Vaudeville. Permanent Address, 114 HANBURY ST., LONDON, N. E. ENG.

"Ricardo Sacco the Fasting Man" who fasted for fifty days only on "water and cigarettes" in a specially constructed glass room at the end of the Arcade. His breakfast meal consisted of eggs and milk. It was reported that 80,000 visitors to the Kursaal came to see him. "The Zulu Warriors" were another great attraction. The "Warriors" were in fact workers at the nearby East India Docks in London who, to supplement their earnings, wore grass skirts and dark make up in order to resemble exotic "Zulus."

Also during the 1929/30 period, while Rameses was appearing at the Kursaal, he was assisted by a youngster named Maurice Fogel. In the early days, Marchinski lived in Hanbury Street, near Chicksand Street in the east end of London where Maurice was born. In fact it was the next street over from Spelman Street, where the Marchinski family had moved to. Maurice's father Nathan was persuaded to put £35 into the Rameses sideshow project at the Kursaal. It was here that this nineteen-year-old would watch avidly and learn how to attract a crowd, how to hold it, and finally how to deliver a show. In the latter days of his run at the Kursaal, Rameses was unable to appear due to serious health issues and perhaps overindulgence to ease the pain, so Maurice had to don the heavy makeup, put on Egyptian garb, and perform the shows himself. With the star's face hidden behind layers of greasepaint, no one was any the wiser.

Those shows were a wonderful training ground for Maurice, not to mention a way for Nathan to secure some sort of return on the "investment" in Marchinski's enterprise. Maurice later said:

> It was here when I first learned about crowd psychology, how to attract a crowd and what to do with them once they had been captured. For every side-show there was always a 'spieler.' It was his job to not only attract the crowd but also gather them

into a small audience. Once 'trapped' they would attract others who were passing by, wondering what was going on.

'Watch the colour watch the eyes of this goose', went the spiel, 'watch the colour, they will turn from red to blue and then to green (no one could see anyway!) Amazing! Before your very eyes ladies and gentlemen I will hypnotise this goose.' It was a verbal attraction to get the crowd interested...[1]

To publicise the show Maurice would often take this goose on a lead for a walk. It was also here (and the Fogel family have confirmed the fact) that Maurice launched his own attraction "A Two Headed Lizard." It was a real lizard, but not two headed. Instead, it had two eyes painted on its tail. P.T. Barnum would have been proud!

In Supreme's magazine *The Magigram* for 1967 an entire issue was devoted to "A Tribute to Fogel." Within that tribute was a column penned by Billy McComb in which he proffered the information that if he were cast adrift onto a desert island with three magicians of his choice, one of them would be Maurice. Even Billy was amazed at Maurice's knowledge of "what must have been an all time complicated illusion." The statement wasn't surprising, considering that Maurice must have had to perform the illusions in the Rameses show many times to keep the production going.

On a visit to Southend in 2008, I was able to find the location of Albert's old house in Essex Terrace and visit the nearby New Empire Theatre he once leased.[2]

Although the building has changed since those heady days, it was inspiring to walk the corridors and steps up onto that same stage that Rameses once walked. The original stage door still exists, as does his old dressing room, number two. ✽

CHAPTER SIX

THE FINAL CURTAIN

ALBERT MARCHINSKI DIED ON Thursday July 31st 1930 in Victoria Hospital Southend. He was only fifty-four years of age. His death certificate stated that the cause of death was (a) post-operative shock due to (b) the removal of colon carcinoma. There was no post-mortem and the certificate was certified by John Myers M.R.C.S. Albert's brother Lesser was noted as next of kin.

In *The Magic Circular* editor Percy Naldrett stated:

> Though not a member of the Circle, 'RAMESES' was well known to magicians and it is with regret that we heard of his death, at Southend in July last. His real name was Albert Marchinsky, as far as we can gather. The show which he used to present was of the apparatus order and consisted mainly of illusions on a brilliantly set stage. Of these, many will recall "Ayesha," considered to be one of the most beautiful levitation acts ever produced. In this the assistant floated gracefully in the air, danced, skipped and otherwise disported herself, and if we remember rightly, she also revolved on a vertical axis, an effect which the writer has not seen before, or since, though we understand it was not original with Rameses. Of late years his show disappeared from the stage and little is known of his subsequent career. He was a landmark, and a kindly soul whose death is sincerely regretted by those who knew him.[1]

Will Goldston had a succinct statement in his *Magician Monthly*:

> **OBITUARY**
> We regret to announce the death of Rameses, who died at Southend Hospital following an operation. His real name was Albert Marchinsky and he had recently been performing at the Southend Kursaal.

The Southend Standard for August 7th 1930 reported:

THE 'GREAT' DEATH OF FAMOUS ILLUSIONIST

A world famous music hall artiste, Albert Rameses, known as 'The Great Rameses' died in the Victoria Hospital, Southend on Thursday, following an operation.

At the beginning of the season Rameses opened an entertainment as an Egyptian illusionist at the Kursaal and had been living with his wife in Grange Gardens, Southend.

In his heyday he was one of the highest paid artistes on the stage and is reputed to have earned as much as £1,000 per week at the London Coliseum. He specialised in Egyptian mysticism. An imposing figure Rameses' portrait was a familiar sight on the theatre advertisement hoardings in London, until more recently, when he fell into somewhat straitened circumstances.

Rameses who was a traveller of world wide experience always kept his real identity a close secret. He was known to his associates as Mr. Rameses, but it is believed that his actual name was Albert Marchinsky. He was associated in more ways than one with Southend, for during the war he was manager of the Old Empire Theatre, which is now The Rivoli Cinema. Though his connection with the theatre was of somewhat short duration he remained a resident of the Borough. At the Mayor's Garden Party this year he was included among the entertainers.

Rameses continued his occupation at the Kursaal to within a week of his fatal illness. He was taken to the Victoria Hospital on the previous Monday and died on Thursday. He leaves a widow, but no children. The remains were conveyed to London on Friday for the funeral.

The Performer, for August 7th wrote:

> Albert Marchinsky, a Russian-Pole, better known to the music-hall profession by his stage name of Rameses, passed away in Southend Hospital on Wednesday last, July 30, following an operation. Rameses, who was 54 years of age, reached the height of his fame nearly 20 years ago, and was recognised as one of the leading illusionists of his day and had toured extensively in Europe and America. At one time he was lessee of the Empire Theatre in Southend, where he had resided for a long time. Of later years he had worked but little on the variety stages of this country, although he had performed locally on various occasions.

The death notice in *The Jewish Chronicle* for August 8th read:

> MARCHINSKY – On the 31st of July, Albert (Great Rameses), eldest son of Eva Marchinsky and the late Phillip Marchinsky, of 9 St Peter's Road, Mile end, passed away at Southend. Deeply mourned by his loving wife, mother, sisters, sisters-in-law, brothers-in-law, relatives and friends. May his dear soul rest in peace.

According to tradition, Albert Marchinski was buried within twenty-four hours in the Jewish Cemetery, Edmonton east London. He was, it seems, not only famous in life but also famous in death for his name appears in the Jewish cemetery register as Albert "Rameses" Marchinski. Such a final billing was a rare honour.

Southend stalwart resident Trudi Couldridge claimed that Albert's widow Mrs. Rosie Rameses was left in dire circumstances after Albert's passing, and was forced to work as a Fortune Teller on Southend Pier to survive. She was also well known for knitting and selling copious woollen garments to make ends meet. Ms. Couldridge has also informed me that Rose Rameses (born Rose Blood) died in 1937 in nearby Rochford, aged sixty-seven.

Maurice Fogel's brother-in-law Maurice Goldhill reported his mother was also a Fortune Teller at the Kursaal so the two women may well have known each other.

Albert had essentially died of colon cancer. His son, Jack Albert, who was born on May 22nd 1900, *also* died at age fifty-five from what was thought be colon cancer. Jack Albert's son Lesser (Lefty Martin) also suffered from colon cancer at that age. Thankfully, however, he is still alive today, living in California.

It was the more detailed recollections of local Southend resident and author Verrall Wass that added much to the discussion. He recalled Marchinksi's St. George's Hall appearances vividly:

> There were five main items if my recollection is correct.
>
> 1 The production of his assistant from miniature pyramids
> 2 An automaton – in reality an assistant suitably dressed and with electric lights decorating his or her? clothes to suggest that the motive power was electricity
> 3 Production of a duck from a 'dove' pan leading into-
> 4 Cremation and restoration of a female assistant
> 5 Asrah – Queen of the Air. This was the version in which the girl assistant floated upwards from a small stool performed various evolutions in the air including skipping. Then, descended to the stool was covered with a cloth, floated upright into the air and then suddenly vanished.

Verrall went on to say:

> Rameses wife was his chief assistant and I believe took part in the Cremation as well as the Levitation.
>
> His stage setting was primarily a black velvet drape. This he used at the Kursaal where only the Duck Pan and the Levitation from his show was performed. The remainder of the entertainment then consisted of smaller effects presented by Maurice Fogel, including, he went on, was the smoothest presentation of the Thirty Card Trick it has been my pleasure to witness.

What struck me most about his (Rameses) performance was the slow pace of his presentation, combined with the simplicity of a master. The slow pace did not mean monotony but the under-lining of every detail of every mystery. While the simplicity meant that only essentials were on stage, that is, each effect was presented as a 'conjuring cameo.' None of the apparatus for the preceding or following effects was allowed on stage.

As will have already been realised, he performed in complete silence.

It was almost so that he met his end. For he knew that he was doomed before he underwent his last operation, and only once did he mention this to me, although I was then seeing him frequently.

I admire him as much for this as for his artistic performance. We could do with more artists – not artistes – of his calibre, artists who think big and are big, artists who do not wish to put their acts in their pockets because it is so much easier than presenting a large show.[2]

Verrall, even though he was knowledgeable, was still baffled by "Ayesha" when he wrote in *The Sphinx*:

'Rameses, the Royal Magician,' is performing at Southend this summer. He is presenting Prof. Harcourt's famous effect, 'Ayesha, Queen of the Air.' The method of working this effect is explained in one of Mr. Goldston's locked books. It is the greatest levitation of the age. I have seen it five times and have not quite got the working. The only apparatus seen is an unprepared stool and, of course, the lady.

He has a young assistant with him who should go far. He has the most finished way of palming cards I have ever seen.

Rameses. Once again here was stoicism in ill-health. Just before he had the operation, after which he died, he spoke to me fatalistically accepting the fact that it was unlikely he would recover. One of his effects I have already described in one of my books. His stage show was divided into three parts presenting only three main effects. These were the burning alive of a girl, an automaton trick, and Harcourt's Flying, and subsequently vanishing, Lady. But each detail of presentation was so carefully studied that the show did not seem a moment too long. His presentation in silence was the reverse of Goldin's in timing. Yet, it attracted by its lack of speed, above all by its simplicity. There are more roads than one to success.[3]

RAMESES, The Great Egyptian Mystic.

courtesy Paul Kieve

Although others worked for Marchinski during his Southend years one can assume that Verrall was referring to Maurice Fogel. Pearl Fogel, Maurice's younger sister, was often sent by train by their mother to Southend with food to ensure that Maurice would not go hungry. Pearl recalled how, as a young and impressionable teenager, she found Marchinski a frightening character. I suppose that out of makeup he would seem a charming man, but in costume and character, with heavy make-up he would have looked very different, especially to a vulnerable young girl.

Marchinski's time at The Kursaal was briefly mentioned in *Maurice Fogel – In Search of The Sensational*. In my research and my innocence I stated that Rameses was unable to work "due perhaps too much liquid at lunch." I may have jumped to the wrong conclusion. Pain controlling drugs were then not what they are today and it could have been that alcohol helped him relive the pain of the cancer from which he was undoubtedly suffering at the time.

Werner Dornfield (1892 – 1982) better known as "Dorny," the National President and then Dean of *The Society of American Magicians* wrote in *The Sphinx*:

> Rameses, the Egyptian Magician. What a show he put on. The only act we ever saw who really 'stopped the show.' Speedy, extravagantly staged and masterfully presented, his was one of the finest illusion acts on the variety stage.[4]

In a later issue of the same journal, Dorny wrote the article 'Thirty Years of Magic Thrills" and said:

> Another big thrill was when I saw the fascinating 'Rameses" from England. He played the Orpheum Circuit and had a lot of bewildering tricks and illusions – mostly original, too. His 'Cremation' was an absolute chef d'ouevre of mysticism. He was the first of the only two magical acts I have ever seen who really stopped the show.[5]

Little was heard of Rameses again in the magic press until 1934 when in the autumn issue of *Goldston's Magical Quarterly* a half page advert appeared: "For Sale 'The Flying Lady'" An illusion that earned him a reputed £100.00 per week!" I do not know whether the illusion was sold, and if so to whom. A letter to Bayard Grimshaw from Arthur Hambling states that he was in the Goldston shop when Cardini, who was appearing at The Palladium at the time, was offered the levitation. He declined.

Although Goldston detailed a "skipping illusion" in his locked book *Exclusive Magical Secrets* earlier in 1912, it should be mentioned that Marchinski was working on perfecting it well before then. Goldston's method was completely impractical for a busy performer like Marchinski.

The first mention of Rameses by Goldston was in *The Magician Annual for 1908-1909*.[6] By the strangest of coincidences on the next page it gives the patent details of Louis Morganstern's "Optical Illusion."[7] It goes on to explain in full detail how to float an actor. This is followed by the details of the "Metallic Corset" that would be needed to effect this floating lady.[8] While the Harcourt or Marchinski method is unknown, we do know that he was using Harcourt's old apparatus. Had Harcourt built it or was it a copy from Carl Hertz?

Harry Latour was a contemporary of Verrall Wass who wrote a letter to Goodliffe's *Abracadabra* that Cecil Lyle had told him "he (Lyle) had bought the levitation from Carmo although he never used it."[9] Lyle, a fellow Vice President in Goldston's Magicians' Club, stated inter alia in an issue of *The Magic Circular* that the illusionist Rameses had been his friend, and he, Lyle, disclosed that Rameses' illusion "Ayesha" was now in his possession.[10] Was Lyle then the mystery buyer of the levitation? According to Granville Taylor, a one-time stage assistant to Lyle, "If Lyle said so it would be more than likely true."

A letter by Tom Waterman published in *The Magic Circular* in 1954 provides key details about the "skipping" piece in "Ayesha":

Dear Editor,

The interest shown by correspondents in the skipping phase of 'Ayesha' as presented by Rameses, leads one to believe that they, like myself, found it distinctly puzzling. The supporting rod, near to its attachment to the lady was encircled by a metal collar which had a socket attached. The floating lady – who was facing right when the cane was handed to her – wedged the right end, which was away from the audience, in the socket and proceeded to skip. All the work was done by her left hand – the right moved in unison but was not in contact with that end of the cane, which travelled round with the collar. The swish of the moving cane added much to the effect, but the audience was not unduly impressed when I saw it. Doubtless many had seen the same illusion worked in sideshows where a hoop was passed downward over the levitated lady. A spring hinged segment at the back of the hoop made this possible. The actual illusion had previously been owned and used by Fred Harcourt, and after his death it was acquired by Rameses.

Sincerely yours,
TOM WATERMAN, A.I.M.C.[11]

Whether or not the method of the illusion was in some way similar to the Carl Hertz patent as detailed in Goldston's *Magician Annual*, it was a complicated piece of machinery to travel with and set up at each venue, to say nothing of the cost of manufacturing and maintenance.[12] Such was the extent of Rameses' commitment to illusion.

In another 1954 issue of *The Magic Circular* Len Webkin inquired about Rameses:

> Contemporary with Lafayette, Chung Ling Soo, Horace Goldin, the Great Carmo and others, there was another. RAMESES, the EGYPTIAN MYSTIC. The name was obviously coined. I remember seeing this act at the Hammersmith Palace, locally known as the Temple, later converted to a cinema. This must have been about 40 to 45 years ago. Although I was then a schoolboy, I had set my heart on being a professional conjurer, and always studied every act I saw very carefully. For this reason I can remember that Rameses wore traditional Egyptian headgear striped in red and white, I believe, with a jewelled cobra ornament in front, flowing robes (wonderful cover, of course) and square beard. I distinctly remember that he made a white horse disappear.
>
> I seem to remember that the presentation was a gorgeous affair, assistants and all the paraphernalia of a big illusion act, but I never read about that particular act anywhere, nor do I find any reference, nor any person that remembers the act.

> Would some of the older members recall this magician? Did some even know him personally? I should be interested (and I feel others might) to hear something about him if any who knew him would vouchsafe the information.
>
> Yours sincerely,
> LEN WEBKIN, M.M.C.
> Low Farm, Kirkleatham, Redcar, Yorks.[13]

The replies came flooding in. Arthur G. Carter offered a reminiscence of seeing the act at St. George's Hall. For him, like many others, the high spot was "Ayesha Queen of the

Air." Percy Naldrett, the editor of *The Magic Circular* and a former employee of The Servais LeRoy Magic Company, recalled seeing the spectacular Rameses show, also recounting that Rameses was the first to use foil confetti. Later he remembered when Rameses was shown a production illusion called "Stolen Jam" at the LeRoy offices. When he was told the price he promptly went away "to think about it" only to make one for a fraction of the cost! Not an uncommon deed during this time period.

Charles Crayford also sang Rameses' praises with a letter:

> Incidentally, as all Members seem to be making a hobby of writing to the Circular about my old and trusted friend Rameses, I may as well fall into line and do likewise. I met this fine performer in his dressing-room at the Hippodrome, Woolwich, S.E., about forty years ago as near as I can remember, when he told me he started in Magic in Africa 'with simple little things like the ink card.' It was a Saturday night when I first saw him and he was very keen on my doing a turn for a pet charity of his the next night somewhere in London, but I was otherwise engaged, so could not oblige. I remember he seemed very delighted when I told him I had seen recently another well-known Illusionist whose levitation I liked very much indeed, but when I added 'I like yours much better, though,' he said, with a smile of satisfaction, 'Oh, so you like mine better, do you?' Rameses was performing at a time when all the other big names in Magic were also filling the Halls, but one must not forget that there was something unlike all the other shows which made the act which Rameses put on stand out in a class of its own, in consequence of which he was always sure of a good house.
>
> Yours faithfully,
> CHAS. CRAYFORD,
> The Kentish Mystic.
> Porth, near Newquay, Cornwall.[14]

A response letter written by Harry Latour mentions a source for some of Rameses' material and addresses Webkin's remark about the disappearance of a white horse:

16th August 1954.

Dear Editor,

In answer to Mr. Webkin in the Magic Circular for August re: Rameses, *The Sphinx* for December 1910, has a short history of Rameses and a photograph on the front cover, and another on the inside page, in costume. His name was Albert Marchinski. I first witnessed Rameses' show at the Empire, Leicester Square, London, about 1909, and quite a few times in later years…

…In Stanyon's 'Explanatory Programmes' will be found his routine, and in a book 'Magician's Road to Fame,' by Laurance Glen – a coloured picture and a few line drawings. I do not remember at any time that Rameses used a white horse in his show.

Perhaps Mr. Webkin is getting mixed up with a show 'The Act Beautiful,' which was a posing act with a white horse, two white dogs with a black background – this was very effective and may have been on the same programme.

I hope this will be of interest to Mr. Webkin.

Yours sincerely,
HARRY LATOUR.
Swiss Cottage, N.W.3 [15]

A letter printed in the August 26th issue describes the mysterious lighting that distinguished the Rameses show from many others:

…I saw RAMESES at the Edinburgh Empire somewhere around 1917 or maybe a year or two later. I can confirm Mr. Webkin's recollection of a big showy illusion act, but alas, details are dimmed by the years.

One strange recollection is the excessive use of blue limelights which no doubt assisted the performer in his mysteries, but left an impression with me that poor visibility was aiding his trickery.

If more details become available, Mr. Editor, I for one would be interested in reading them.

Sincerely,
BRUCE POSGATE, A.I.M.C.
Toronto, Canada.

It seems that Mr. Webkin had brought in a flurry of replies all praising Rameses' work.

An entry in the magazine *Encore* provided brief rhymes of praise:

A wonderful man is Rameses
Whose fame every season increses
With his magical art
He does well from the start
And your interest never ceases [16]

After this, however, all went quiet again. Little, if anything, has been written of the great Egyptian Wonderworker since then. Marchinski seems to have been forgotten. Even Milbourne Christopher's highly detailed *The Illustrated History of Magic* fails to mention him. Considering the success that Marchinski found in his own time, the omission of his name from the annals of conjuring seems a sad end to an otherwise bright light of conjuring's golden age. ❋

CHAPTER SEVEN

❧ THE LOST RELATIVES

IN 1989, totally out of the blue, the postman brought me a letter from San Diego, California. It came as a most pleasant surprise. It was from a Mrs. Margaret Doser who said she was the granddaughter of Albert Marchinski, who she was beginning to research. Jay Marshall had suggested she write to me, possibly as a result of the Fogel connection. In her subsequent letters, she sent me photocopies of relevant pages that had been kindly sent to her by Dr. Edwin Dawes. She had been in touch with him since visiting her local library where she discovered a copy of *The Great Illusionists*.

Margaret and I corresponded for quite some time but, strangely, in 1991 my last letter to her address was returned as "address not known." I assumed that either she had neglected to file a change of address with the post office, or that she had died.

This was all long before I gained access to the world wide web.

Some ten years later, with Richard Mark, I set about completing the Maurice Fogel biography. While I was researching the Marchinski/Fogel connection, Max Maven told me that the two were blood relatives. He had learned this from Maurice himself. With newly available technology, I once again attempted to trace Margaret, but to no avail.

In the intervening months I had been in contact by email with three different UK sources all setting out their family history and connections with Marchinski. It seemed they were related. Things were heating up on the "detective" front, and all three said there was an "American connection." At this point I confirmed that the famous Hollywood-based singer Tony Martin was really Tony Marchinski, a relation, but that was all.

I had also recently spoken to Arnold Shaffer, an eighty-two-year-old member of Maurice Fogel's family, who lives in my hometown of Bournemouth. He recalled, as a five-year-old child, being taken to the Kursaal in Southend to see a magician sometime between 1929 and 1930. All he could remember was that the magician was "Egyptian." Maurice Fogel worked for Marchinski in the 1929 period. So perhaps Mr. Shaffer was being taken to see his uncle Maurice.

In the interim, an archive website had had been set up by the Empire Theatre once owned by Marchinski. At about the same time, I received an email from a lady in Texas who turned out to be the great-granddaughter of Albert Marchinski! I was on the trail again and happy to learn that "auntie" Margaret Doser had not died but had moved without telling me.

An invitation to the Los Angeles Conference on Magic History was too good an opportunity to miss, and a further drive south to a San Diego suburb allowed me to meet Margaret. It seems there were seven children who were born to Jack Albert Martin, the son of Albert, five of whom are still living. The direct relatives often "Anglicised" their surname, changing it to Martin or sometimes March. Jack Albert had married Adelaide Maria (Marty) Hubert, a young native of Guernsey. Because Jack was Jewish and Adelaide was not, they both became the black sheep of their families. In search of a new life, the couple left London and moved to Toronto, Canada where they married on October 28th 1922. Jack was a talented theatre scene painter in that area, and some of his work remains in use to this day.

Upon arriving in the San Diego area, my first call was to Margaret. She seemed dazed by my telephone call, perhaps never expecting to hear from me. On a sunny afternoon my wife Nadine and I met her, and at last I was able to put a face with all the letters I had received and fortuitously kept all those years ago. Margaret was a charming lady who seemed just as thrilled as me by the meeting.

A day or so later I made an appointment to meet her brother Lesser, better known as "Lefty", the eldest in the family, a sprightly eighty-two years young. We met for breakfast and we chatted and chatted. I knew there was more information now that the ball was rolling.

Lefty, now retired, had had an exciting career and is still well known in drag-racing circles as a "bit of a daredevil." Another showman, if only on the race-track, and another piece of the puzzle.

In 2007, during a talk on the Palladium, a lady named Philippa Brauer happily greeted me with "I have a relative of Rameses in the USA." After another meeting in 2008, Philippa put me in touch with her sister-in-law Aida who lives in Florida and after an exciting and lengthy telephone call it appeared that I had made someone else very happy by putting them in contact with distant relatives. Aida, the great niece of Albert, recalled that her aunt Pearl, Albert's sister, often recounted how thrilled the family was by the success of the Rameses Show: when Albert came home from a long tour they would shower him with gold sovereigns. Pearl also vividly remembered Houdini visiting their London home many times when he was in town.

In 2009, I had the great pleasure of presenting "Rameses – The Forgotten Star" at the 11th Los Angeles Conference on Magic History. Following my talk, I was thrilled that Lesser "Lefty" Martin was there to take a bow on behalf of his grandfather. As so often happens, additional information comes to light directly following my talks. Collectors and historians have a well-deserved reputation for generosity. Max Maven kindly proffered the important detail (given to him by Maurice Fogel) that the arch surrounding the black cave where the skipping illusion took place was painted bright white in order to act as a "blinder."

Rameses' passion for his craft was the driving force that kept him going. Even after the Southend theatre disaster in 1917/1918 he carried on working and reinventing himself. Not because he had to, but because he wanted to. Make no mistake, working twice nightly on variety shows made for a tough existence even when you were top of the bill.

Life is a mystery in itself. A mystery all on its own. Over these past months of research the big mystery for me has been, and will always be, Rameses disappearance from the historical record. When I first undertook this project it was like imagining the full picture of a jigsaw puzzle with only a few pieces. This journey has been a fascinating one for me, sometimes bordering on obsession, because I dearly would have wished to have met the man or have at least seen him in action.

Melodrama is a word that comes to mind when I imagine the overall impression of Rameses' show. My own dictionary defines a "melodrama" as: "A sensational dramatic piece with violent appeals to the emotions and a happy ending." This could most certainly have been written with the Rameses show in mind! In short, you could say he was a *showman*! The Yiddish theatre that he began in must have influenced his style of performance. The heavy make up being only part of his Egyptian persona. But the reviews (both by magicians and the laity) all agree that the show was a colourful and flamboyant whirlwind, qualities sometimes missing from today's theatrical magic shows.

One could always debate how good Marchinski's work actually was, but amidst countless enthusiastic reviews, the only adverse criticism I could find, if that is indeed what it was, came from Peter Warlock in one of his *New Pentagram* "Talkback" columns where he made the rather mild criticism:

> Strange that so many magicians who have adopted an oriental role have used effects that in no way could be attributed to oriental magicians. Even Rameses with so much of his act pointed Egyptian-wise had to introduce the pierrot automaton.[1]

But Martin Beck would never have rebooked the Rameses North American tour in 1913 if the first trip in 1910 had not been a success. Beck's wise decision to book him in the first instance in 1910 obviously paid dividends for both of them.

Perhaps the greatest proof of Rameses' mastery can be found in his words of advice to fellow performers:

TO POTENTIAL CONJURERS
by RAMESES

I have no knowledge of the degrees by which a tightrope walker or a steeplejack attains proficiency. But I do not suppose that one would start tight-rope walking by attempting to cross the Niagara Falls, still less, to run across; or the other begin by climbing to the top of a factory chimney. Creep before you can walk is a law of nature.

The beginner desirous of becoming a conjurer would save himself much disappointment with his performances if he could be persuaded to exercise some patience in the initial stages, thereby laying the foundation of good habits on which his 'show' could surely, if slowly, go on improving, until the most had been made of his capabilities.

It is admitted that conjuring is a gift – conjuring, that is to say, of a superior quality. But, assuming the absence of this gift – and the possession of it had better be ignored – it is, broadly speaking, possible for all to attain proficiency by taking 'pains.' By 'pains' is not here meant hard and laborious practise. On the contrary, even painstaking practise can become a real pleasure, if pursued in the real, hopeful spirit.

Many beginners manifest too great a desire to show off tricks before they have been thoroughly mastered in private. One could cite instances of conjurers who never trouble to practise at all. Their methods being wrong fundamentally, doom them to chronic mediocrity, or still worse than that, a parallel in their case is that of a traveler who, having taken the wrong turning, finds himself further out of the beaten track with every step he takes.

It has always seemed a funny thing to me that people beginning conjuring, should overlook the need for a preparatory course. That they should start performing when they think they have the rudiments of a few tricks, evidently presuming that, unlike any other hobby or profession, magical entertaining can be done not only without taking pains, but even without taking thought.

Hundreds of magical entertainers are in this tantalising predicament to-day. One day showing, 'respectably for me,' as they say, or the next, 'as awkward as an owl,' though why the nocturnal bird of prey should be dragged into this comparison, I don't know, unless it be for its doleful hoot, or daylight blindness whereby it is unable to open its eye to the need for doing a thing properly.

I think it will be unanimously agreed that ordinary work a day brains will be found sufficient to enable anybody with the requisite limbs and senses to give a decent conjuring act – providing their early conjuring education has been satisfactorily attended to, and that is what I am coming to in real earnest.

Begin at the bottom, and of this be sure – the early stages are thoroughly pleasurable, so long as you do not chafe too much to be up on the platform and doing a "show."

This counsel is for your good. You will write me a letter of thanks on giving your first performance after taking a patient preparatory course of three months; preferably six, if your stock of patience and your capacity for taking pains can run to it.

The great desideratum is that the beginner should learn how to perform the various sleights smoothly, also acquire an easy, still, and if possible, a pleasant personality.

That is the Alpha and Omega of magical entertaining and indeed the whole art of the wonderful game. ✺

❧ CONCLUSION

IF I HAVE ONE REGRET in the whole Marchinski saga it is that there is no moving image of Albert either at work or play. Not only is there no moving image, but the music that he used remains unknown. Quite a lot happened during the show that would have been punctuated with the appropriate music and accompanying chords and cymbal crashes.

It must be said that Marchinski's elaborate Egyptian costume of fiery red velvet with golden accessories and purple cape, and with his ornate head-dress, must have made for a formidable character, and combined with full heavy makeup, an impressive sight to behold. At 5' 7" one couldn't say he was exactly tall by today's standards, and he was slight of build, so he must have compensated with his agility on the stage, giving his movements an air of authority.

Following the wonderful and memorable charity Matinee Royal Gala in aid of the Chelsea Hospital for Women at the Palladium in 1914, there was an afternoon garden party at the hospital the following day given as a "thank you" to all the artists. It was filmed, or so I have been led to believe, but as yet no one can find that film. I don't know if Albert or his wife and brothers attended, but it would be wonderful to see nevertheless.

I wonder if the film still exists?

We are bombarded today with moving imagery, whether it is via television, cinema, computers, or even mobile phones. It is such a shame that future generations will never be able to see exactly what Rameses or his illusion show was really like. While we might know the color of his eyes and how tall he was, we don't know how he conducted himself, how he walked or talked. Although it would have been a silent film and his well-travelled act was silent too, it would have been wonderful to watch nevertheless. So with only the written evidence it is like having a two-dimensional character, almost like one would get on radio where you are allowed to paint your own picture.

I hope that these few words that I have put together on the exciting life of Albert Marchinski, a fighter if ever there was one, will enable you, the reader, to put together your own moving image of his life and career. From the humblest of beginnings, living in the poorest part of London, he ended his life in a Palace, albeit a "Palace of Illusions." Hopefully in his eyes he had succeeded in everything he set out achieve.

Finally, and as fate would have it, some eight years ago my daughter married into a family that had, would you believe, a Marchinski in the family tree! Serendipity is such a beautifully descriptive and meaningful word, don't you think? Other Marchinskis are seemingly coming out the woodwork since my excursion into his past. One day I hope to meet even more of the clan.

With so much new information that we do know now about Rameses there are still many things we don't: where exactly he was born; where he went to school; when he and his parents left Korvno; what he was like as a person.

Maybe we will never know.

Maybe this is all part of the Rameses mystery.

I'll hope to address some of those issues before the curtain falls.

❧ POSTSCRIPT

Apart from finding a racehorse in Australia named Magic Albert and another named Marchinski, and a Psycadelia LP sleeve utilizing the well known Butterfly poster within five miles of my home, there is a pop group called — would you believe it? — "Rameses" that has played Southend on a number of occasions.

It was Jeanette Marchinski who informed me that Yehudi Menuhin and Sandow the strongman were also on the family tree.

A company called Spooky Locations recently scheduled an event at the New Empire Theatre in Southend. They have hired the building for a night to try and contact ghosts from the past. I wonder if they managed to contact Albert?

Just as this manuscript was being finalized a thoughtful gift came to me from John Fisher — a pack of Rameses cards. These were not only playing cards with a delightful Rameses picture on their backs but also "Fortune Telling Cards." This prompted me to search more into their age and background. Would you believe they were manufactured by Chas Goodall and Company of Camden London in 1910? Nothing strange in that, but this was the same year that Albert hit the headlines in London with his Coliseum appearance where he was spotted by Beck, a meeting that would lead to his first US Orpheum tour. Albert also appeared by coincidence in 1910 in Camden. Until further evidence comes to light to say otherwise I would like to think it too much of a coincidence that someone from the Chas Goodall playing card factory could well have issued these delightful gilt edged cards as result of either seeing Rameses show or after a conversation with Albert himself.

RAMESES IN PRINT

What follows are a collection of tricks and comments made by Rameses in British magical journals. Though frequently the subject of conversation in print, Marchinski seldom played the role of author. The examples that follow explain a bit of his thinking as a performer, as well as his style of writing, and the kind of magic that appealed to him. Each piece was written by Marchinski, though the bylines in every case credited him as, simply, "Rameses."

❡ GET OUTS

(*Magic Wand* p.115 1928)

Occasionally the unpleasant individual who will have his own way when supposedly 'helping' a performer makes himself a positive nuisance. It is advisable to ignore those gentry whenever possible, but sometimes they are too persistent to be conveniently overlooked. They demand to do all sorts of things in their efforts to trap the conjurer, and if they are too openly ignored, sit back in smug satisfaction, and announce to all and sundry, 'Ah, he was afraid to let me shuffle the pack. He couldn't catch me.'

These folks are luckier than they realize, if the wizards wand was a solid bar of steel instead of a light affair of wood, magic would receive a free advertisement in all the Sunday newspapers. It is usually card tricks on which such people expend their best efforts. They know all about 'Forcing and all that tricky business, don't you know.' It always amuses me to see them deliberately take a card either actually from the top or second down. Poor mights, I always make a point of noting the bottom, and top two cards, when dealing with them, and it often comes off.

Sometimes, however, on the spur of the moment, one has to do some pretty rapid thinking, and it is always advisable to take a leaf out of the Boys Scouts code, and BE PREPARED. Here are one or two 'get outs' that I always keep at the back of my mind. Some time ago, after showing some card effects, that 'although I say it who shouldn't,' were really good, an individual said 'Can I examine the cards?' On my handing them to him for this purpose, he gave them a thorough shuffle, picked out a card, showed it to his neighbour, shuffled the card back into the pack, and handed it back to me. 'Now,' he cried triumphantly 'tell me what card I selected.' I ask you! The patron saint of magicians I know not, but he was with me. I had what my old 'Guvnor' Harry Tate-would call a "rush of brains to the head." I went to my bag to fetch a silk handkerchief. At any rate I returned with one. "What was your card?" I enquired." Nine of Spades," was the reply. The pack was duly wrapped up in the handkerchief, and the Nine of Spades appeared in the approved fashion.

In my bag I had a pair of fakes for producing any card called for, and they were all set. Further explanation is superfluous.

Another get out is to inquire the name of the card, and count the number of letters there are in the name. For instance, the Four of Clubs being the card, the performer notes that there are eleven letters. Fan the cards, asking the spectator to see that his card is still in the pack, and locate it. If the performer is an adept at thumb counting he can dispense with the fanning, locating the card by glimpsing the index of each card as it is released by the thumb.

Having spotted the card he now counts one less than the number of letters (which in this case is ten) above it, makes a break, and when apparently squaring up the cards, he inserts his little finger at the break. Turning to another spectator he requests him to cut the pack, and forces the cut at the break. The selected card is now the eleventh card down in the pack.

If the performer prefers, he can of course cut the cards himself, either openly or by means of the pass, but the former method is the best. The spectator is now instructed to spell out the name of his card, removing a card for each letter a la the old Spelling Bee trick, and then the final letter will be his card.

Another suggestion which I read in an American book so amused me that one night I tried it to see what would happen, and was amazed at the result.

Someone had refused a force, and then demanded that he might return the card to the pack himself. Our old friend 'the Crimp' is a very handy asset and I was just going to employ this subterfuge, when the suggestions I had read occurred to me, I followed them to the letter, purely as stated, out of curiosity. 'What was your card? ' I demanded.

'Seven of Hearts,' was the reply.

Turning impressively to the audience I announced 'Seven of Hearts. Quite correct.'

It was fully half a minute before they realised they had been spoofed, and when the laugh came, it was a laugh with me, and no more was heard from the wise guy, who looked somewhat bewildered and I am convinced was not quite sure in his own mind exactly what had happened. However, just to give him the 'coup de grace,' I worked Merlin's 'Spread' on him, and in the language of the poets, that put the tin hat on it.

Another handy asset is a carbon pad. The name of the card may be written down, and the writer tears the paper up, or puts it in his pocket, and there you are.

Then there is the time honoured device of (having been informed the name of the card) boldly asserting that it is not in the pack at all. Then proving (?) this by running through the cards, finding- it quicker than the spectator and palming it into the pocket. This 'get out' is greatly improved if the performer can manage to secretly introduce the card into the spectator's pockets. It is often possible to glimpse a card when in the spectator's hands, I personally, do not announce that I have seen the card, and have another card selected. Instead, by reason of my accidental information, I present some apparent miracle. The conjurer's aim is to discover in nearly all card tricks, the selected card. Why, then, should he take the trouble to use all sorts of artifices if the careless spectator presents him with this information free, gratis, and for nothing. 'All's fair in Conjuring,' the performer's raison d'etre is to deceive entertainingly. The element of surprise is a great factor in magic, and it is this very element that sometimes momentarily disconcerts the inexperienced magician. By being prepared for all contingencies, the astute performer can emerge from apparent difficulties with flying colours. Fortunately these 'get outs' are not often required as such, for 'know alls' are greatly in the minority, and only crop up occasionally, but when they do it is always satisfactory to be fully prepared for all their "traps," and to smilingly "flatten them out," to the general relief of everyone.

⚐ 12 CARDS TO POCKET
(*Magic Wand* p.165 1928)

The only excuse I make for introducing this old effect is the fact that in no book on conjuring have I ever seen a proper explanation of the essential moves of the trick.

The moves I refer to are the means by which the cards are palmed preparatory to their being introduced into the pocket. Most manuals merely state baldly that so many cards are palmed. Admittedly the said manual may also teach palming, but I venture to suggest that palming as explained therein can never be applicable to the above effect.

I will endeavour to explain more fully. Supposing a card manipulator desires to place this effect in his programme (and it is a trick worthy of any student of card conjuring), how is he going to produce the experiment in a finished manner from the bare description, 'Here palm off six cards, etc.?' Those cards have to be palmed off cleanly, quickly, and in such a manner that, not even a person aware of what is happening, can say he actually saw the performer palm the cards. The following moves will, I think, appeal to everyone who has essayed this pretty effect.

First, let me give (as the late Professor Hoffman would have said) the bare bones of the trick. The performer counts off twelve cards into his right hand. These cards are transferred to the left hand while the right empties the right hand trouser pocket. The lining of the pocket is replaced, the cards in the left hand click, and a card is brought out of the previously empty pocket. This goes on until four, five, or six cards have been produced from the pocket. The cards in the left hand are then counted to prove that the cards in the pocket have actually left the hand. Again the cards are placed in the left hand, which clicks them rapidly, and three cards are produced in a fan from pocket. The last three cards are placed in the left hand, from whence they vanish, and once more are brought out of the right-hand trouser pocket. Now for the moves referred to. The left hand holds the pack and the left thumb pushes off the cards into the right hand while performer counts one, two, etc. On coming to seven, the seventh card, is placed on top as usual, except that the bottom of the card is nearly a third of the way up from the bottom of the six already in the hand. The other five are counted on to the seventh. (See Fig. 1.)

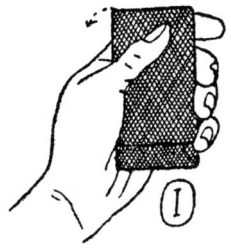

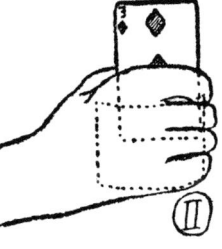

There must be no hesitation in counting. The twelve cards are counted out rapidly as they are transferred from the pack to right hand. The cards are then taken in the left hand, the remainder of the pack having been placed aside. The right hand is shown empty, and the cards transferred from left to right for the purpose of showing the left. In transferring the cards back to the left hand the move is made. As the left hand approaches the right, the fingers of the right hand bear on the six cards which jut out, thus pressing them into the palm. The left hand then places the remaining cards between the fingers and thumb of the right hand. (See Fig. 2.)

With a little practice this move may be accomplished so quickly and neatly that not even a conjurer would be aware that the cards had been palmed. Next place the cards into the left hand, explaining what you intend doing and then turn out the right trouser pocket. (If performer thinks fit, there is no need, in my opinion, to use the pocket dodge.) Keeping the cards in the right hand, turn out the pocket, replace, and then put in the six cards. As I am explaining my method, I will not go into details regarding alternative ways of doing this, but it must be remembered it should be presented just as the performer desires.

To resume. The performer clicks the cards in the left hand and brings out one card from his pocket. Another, and yet another click, and now three cards have been disclosed (each card is, dropped on to the table as it is produced).

On clicking for the fourth card, the conjurer looks perplexed and -dives about his pocket. This gives him the opportunity to palm a fourth card from his pocket. He then pats his body as if feeling for card, and eventually reproduces it from under the arm, at the same time looking relieved, and remarking, "Sometimes it gets stuck half-way." The fifth card is extracted normally, after which the six in the left hand are counted as seven. Another click and the sixth card is produced, after which the cards in the left hand are again counted, this time properly, and found to number six. When counting the six cards, they are placed as in the first part of the experiment, viz., the three top cards overlapping. The same moves are gone through in placing the cards into the pocket, after which the cards in the left hand are clicked three times rapidly. The right hand is then shown empty, it dives into pocket and produces the three cards in a fan.

For the last three cards, the left hand is slightly curled, back to audience, with the palm facing the body, which latter is turned almost left side on to the front of the stage. The cards are placed between the left forefinger and thumb and the right hand, palm upwards, with the backs of fingers, pushes the cards downwards into the left hand. As the right hand pushes the cards down, however, they are back palmed in the right hand. The left hand then moves away from body as if containing the cards, and the performer turns his right side on to audience, at the same time front palming the cards in the right hand, Both hands are then shown, fingers wide apart (merely doubling up the cards in the right and clipping them with the thumb). Finally, the right hand travels over to the right pocket and extracts the three cards. The last move may seem complicated, and hardly feasible, but try it! It is the method I have always used, and I may say I never do anything in public which is not practical or mystifying.

As I have already mentioned, there is no necessity to work the effect exactly as explained. Every performer has his own method. But I do think, and so do many others to whom I have shown my moves, that they are the quickest and cleanest for this particular trick.

The effect should be worked as quickly as possible. I do not mean rushed through, of course, but with no hesitation or unnecessary "talkee-talkee," The speed will come with practise.

I think it is hardly necessary to add that this effect should always be followed by the diminishing cards.

♣ DIMINISHING CARDS
(*Magic Wand* p.145 1928)

Although one of the oldest of card tricks this effect is undoubtedly one of the finest extant. I have worked it at cabarets, clubs, and some of the largest halls in the country. It is one of the very few effects which can be performed in every sphere of conjuring activity. The effect briefly is as follows.

The performer has five cards, which he fans. He turns over his hand (the cards being in view all the time), and turns his pocket inside out to prove that it is empty. Now, blowing on the cards, they are found to be reduced to half their former size.

They can be shown separately if necessary. The first move is repeated and the cards are found to have diminished to one-quarter of their original size. They may be examined if necessary. The cards are then placed in the left hand, a rubbing motion is executed, and cards have vanished. They are finally extracted from right hand trousers, pocket, as the conjurer remarks, " Restored to their original condition."

METHOD AND PRESENTATION.

The five full-size cards are already on table, together with the half-size cards, the latter king behind the former (Fig. 1.) and all being face upwards. Fan, keeping the hands well away from the body and then close cards. The right hand squares up the cards, palms off large ones and leaves the half-size behind in left hand. The left hand, as right moves away, turns over so that the thumb is towards floor and the back of hand is towards the audience. (Fig. 2.) As the greater portion of half-size packet is still in view, there is nothing to distinguish these cards from the larger ones. At this point the pocket is turned inside out with the right hand, which latter leaves the cards in the upper portion of the pocket. The left hand swings round, fanning cards, which are found to have been reduced to half their former size. Simultaneously the

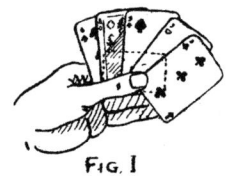

Fig. I

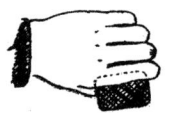

Fig. II

right hand obtains possession of the packet of quarter-size cards, which were vested on the right hand side (or alternatively, concealed under the right lapel). If working at close quarters this move can be deferred until the cards are being examined. To produce the quarter-size cards, repeat the above movements, and on bringing the hand away with half-size cards, remark something as follows:- "They are now almost small enough to travel up the sleeve, across the body and into the pocket. First, however, I shall make them smaller still to prevent jamming." The right hand, with cards palmed, describes the motions exactly as related. On reaching the word 'body,' the right hand, which is then at the left side, throws the cards into a (Harold Comden's) 'Topit' vanisher, never hesitating for a moment in going across the body to the right hand trouser pocket. The right hand, by the time it reaches the pocket, should have the fingers wide apart: Slowly showing hand empty, the performer now tucks in his pocket. (Leaving the pocket hanging out until this stage, I consider very effective.) Now the left hand, which has the lower half of the half-size (?) cards still in view, is turned over and the cards are found to be smaller still. They can be made even smaller, of course, by Robert Houdin's method, but this I think, is superfluous. The small cards are now displayed in the right hand. The right hand approaches left, palms the cards, and the movements are continued exactly as with the half-size cards. Meanwhile the left hand executes a rubbing motion. When the right hand has been shown empty the left slowly opens, the right hand at same time going to the pocket and extracting the cards as the performer states "Restored to their original condition."

(For cabaret, where one is invariably surrounded, the hands are kept palms downwards. Otherwise the movements are the same. The right hand must necessarily be kept close to body. As the pocket is turned inside out, the body swings to the left, which permits of the larger cards being placed inside.)

If you do not possess a 'Topit' vanisher I recommend you to buy or make one immediately. It is undoubtedly one of the handiest props extant. I am convinced that once you have tried the above method, the 'Diminishing cards' will become one of the stand-bys of your repertoire. I have been complimented innumerable times on this effect and although I never conjure to conjurers, I have puzzled dozens by the above method. I think the mere fact of showing each card separately gives the trick a new lease of life. Many people who have seen me work this, afterwards remarked, 'I thought the cards folded up, but yours, apparently, do not'. Which shows that the public are more or less aware of the old method of working this effect. Then again, never approaching a table or picking up other cards to show their comparative size (as in the Bertram method) still further confuses the mind of the onlooker.

Only one point more; no matter how easy this is, and it is easy, give it plenty of practice before attempting to show it. If there are any points on which you are not quite clear, I shall be only too pleased to unravel them on receipt of a letter explaining exactly what it is you do not understand.

CHRONOLOGY
A TIMELINE OF RAMESES PERFORMANCES AND EVENTS

1908
October 5 Islington Hippodrome London.

1909
January 25 Empire Theatre, Dame Street Dublin
June 21 Royal Hippodrome Liverpool for the week
September 20 Grand Theatre Nelson Lancashire

1910
April 15 Albert was initiated into the Chelsea Masonic Lodge.
April Kilburn Empire
February 28 London Coliseum
The Tour opened in **July 31** Denver Colorado.

October 31 on the Orpheum Circuit Salt Lake City
November 7 Ogden Utah
November 14 Denver
December 12 Omaha
December 19 Minneapolis
December 26 St Paul

1911
January 1 Majestic Theatre Milwaukee
January 8 Chicago
January 15 St Louis
January 23 Indianapolis
February The tour closed on February 12th in New Orleans and after making their way back to New York they sailed back to the UK on **March 8 1911**
April 3 Palladium

April 10 Shoreditch Olympia
April 17 Poplar Hippodrome
May 1 Empire Theatre Stockport
May 8 Regent Theatre Salford
May 15 Shepherd's Bush Empire
May 27 Inaugural Meeting at the Magicians' Club
August 7 Empire Theatre Bristol
September 18 Margate Hippodrome.
September 25 Holborn Empire

1912
February n.d. Canning Town Imperial Theatre
March 11 Shoreditch Olympia Theatre
March 18 Willesden Hippodrome
July 15 Palladium
July 22 Kilburn Empire
August 19 Burnley Palace
September 2 Chiswick Empire Theatre
September 9 Wood Green Empire (he was paid £50.00.)
September 23 Coliseum
1912 Holborn Empire
October Coliseum
December New Theatre Northampton
December Blackburn Royal

1913
1913 Edmonton

June 21 'Albert Rameses' along with his wife Rosie arrived in New York

1914
March 16 London Palladium
March 17 A ROYAL MATINEE
March 22 Rameses, Lesser and Albert Simmons visited Will Goldston's Magicians' Club.
August 31 Aldershot Hippodrome

1915
February 22 Holborn Empire
April 5 London Palladium
1915 See M.M. Vol X # 5 April 1915
August 16 Norwich Hippodrome
December 13 Brighton Hippodrome

1916
February 22 Leeds Hippodrome
April 24 Aldershot Hippodrome
November 13 Norwich Hippodrome
December 4 Islington Empire
December 11 Rameses Holborn Empire

1917
August Albert takes a lease on Empire Theatre Southend
June 4 Aldershot Hippodrome
August September Kingston Empire

October 29 Holborn Empire

November Holborn Empire

1918

April 8 Southend ticket

November 4 London Palladium

November 11 London Palladium

1919

January 6 Leicester Palace Theatre (January 11 salary paid £70)

January 20 London Palladium

August 4 Coliseum

August Empire Theatre Birmingham

September 15 South Shields Empire

October 27 Leicester Palace Theatre (Salary paid £70)

1920

January 26 Coliseum.

February 2 Chatham Empire Theatre Of Varieties (Salary paid £65.00)

January February Manchester Hippodrome

March 8 Leicester Palace Theatre (Salary paid £70.00)

November Empire theatre Chatham (£70.00 salary receipt)

December 20 Wood Green Empire (Salary paid £58.6.8d)

December 27 Bristol Hippodrome

1921

January 3 Leicester Place Theatre (Salary paid January 8 £75.00)

1923

March 5 The Alhambra Leicester Square

September 4-week season at St Georges Hall

October 5 St. George's Hall

October 12 St. George's Hall

1924

February 22 St. George's Hall

February 29 St. George's Hall

March 7 St. George's Hall

March 15 Review of current season in the *Magical News*

1928

During the 1928/9/30 period Rameses appeared at the Kursaal Southend on Sea Essex. One of his assistants was a young Maurice Fogel.

1930

July 31st, Thursday Albert Marchinski dies in Victoria Hospital Southend, and the following day is buried in the Federation Synagogue burial grounds, Edmonton.

SOURCES

Bamberg, Theo with Robert Parish. *Okito on Magic*. Edward O. Drane, 1952.

Crowe, Ken. *Kursaal Memories*. Oxfordshire: Joyland Books, 2003.

Davenport, Anne and John Salisse. *St. Georges Hall*. Pasedena: Mike Caveney's Magic Words, 2001.

Dawes, Edwin A. *The Great Lyle*. Pasedena: Mike Caveney's Magic Words, 2005.

Dawes, Edwin. *The Magic of England*. 1984.

Dawes, Edwin. *The Great Illusionists*. David & Charles, 1979.

Glen, Laurance. *The Magicians Road to Fame*. Ludo Press, 1922.

Llanes, Ricardo M. *Teatros de Buenos Aires*. no. XXVIII of the series Cuadernos de Buenos Aires, 1968.

Lewis, Eric and Peter Warlock. *P.T. Selbit*. Pasedena: Mike Caveney's Magic Words, 1989.

Price, David. *Magic: A Pictorial History of Conjurers in the Theater*. Cornwall Books, 1985.

Reynolds, Charles and Regina. *A Hundred Years of Magic Posters*. London: Darien House, 1975.

Skues, Keith. *That's Entertainment : 100 Years Chelsea Lodge No 3098*, 2005.

Taylor, Granville. *Wonders Never Cease*. Published privately.

Wass, Verrall. *Astound Your Audience Volume Two.* 1936.

Woodward, Chris and Richard Mark. *Maurice Fogel: In Search of The Sensational.* Seattle: Hermetic Press, 2007.

Woodward, Chris. *The London Palladium: The Story of The Theatre and its Stars.* Jeremy Mills Publishing, 2008.

Periodicals:

Abracadabra

The Budget

Genii Conjurers Magazine

The Magic Circular

Felsman's Magical Review

Goldston's Magician Monthly

The Linking Ring

Servais le Roy's Magical Monthly

The Magigram

The Pentagram

New Pentagram

The Performer

The Sphinx

Sterling's Magical World

The Wizard

Tit-Bits

The Era

The Thistle

ENDNOTES

PROLOGUE

[1] *Magician Monthly* (vol. 13), p. 118.

CHAPTER ONE

[1] Hatton, Henry. *The Sphinx* (vol. 9, no. 10), p. 211.

CHAPTER TWO

[1] Eleven years on still, your author would also make an appearance on that same stage!

[2] *The Sphinx* (vol. 8), p.128.

[3] *Magician Monthly* (October 1909).

[4] *Stanyon's* (vol. 10, June 1910), p. 68.

[5] *Sterling's Magic World* (vol. 1, no. 17, February 1911).

[6] Wilson, *Magazine of Wonder*

[7] Hatton, Henry., *The Sphinx* (vol. 9, no. 10), p. 211.

[8] *Kansas City Star* (1910)

[9] *Sphinx* (1910), p. 257.

[10] *The Demon Telegraph* (no. 91).

[11] An identical review appeared in *Sterling's Magic World* (May 1911).

[12] *The Magic Mirror* (June 1912) p.49

[13] *Cape Times Newspaper* (April 1912)

[14] *Magician Monthly* (September 1912).

[15] *L'Illusioniste* (March and June 1913)

[16] *Salt Lake Telegram* (November 11 1911).

[17] *The Magic Wand* (vol. 6), p. 180.

[18] *Sterling's Magic World*, p.100.

[19] *Goldston Annual of Magic* (no. 29)

[20] *The Magic Wand* (vol. 4, March 1914), p. 682.

[21] There were sadly so many questions I could have asked Maurice Fogel and should have, but regrettably never did. I vividly recall him discussing illusions with me and specifically the Rameses skipping in mid air illusion. He asked me if I knew how it was done and I gave a brief description one that I had seen in an early Goldston book. Regrettably I never thought to take the discussion further. How was I to know that one day I would write about Maurice, and later still become totally absorbed by his mentor Mr. Marchinski?

[22] *The Press* (1914).

[23] *The Standard* (1914).

[24] *The Referee* (1914).

[25] *The Magic Wand* (June 1914).

[26] *The Aldershot Review* (August 1914).

[27] *The Magic Wand* (vol. 5), p. 57.

[28] *Magician Monthly* (vol. 11), p. 38.

[29] *Magician Monthly* (vol. 10, no. 5, April 1915).

[30] *Magician Monthly* (April 1915).

[31] *The Magic Circular* (1915)

[32] *Magician Monthly* (1917 vol. 13, no. 12, November) p.182.

CHAPTER THREE

[1] *The Performer (*1915)

[2] *Magician Monthly* (vol. 13) p. 118.

[3] *The Southend Telegraph* (October 26th 1918).

[4] *The Southend Telegraph* (July 26th 1919).

[5] *The Sphinx* (April 1920).

CHAPTER FOUR

[1] Farelli, Victor. *The Pentagram* (1951).

[2] *The Gazette* (December 31st 1920).

[3] *Magician Monthly* (vol. 19), p. 113.

[4] *Magician Monthly* (vol. 20, no. 2).

[5] Young, John. *The Magic Circular.*

[6] *Magician Monthly* (1929).

[7] *The Magic Wand* (1928).

[8] Wass, Verrall. *Astound You Audience* (1936).

CHAPTER FIVE

[1] Maurice Fogel

[2] Once in the theatre foyer it was spooky to see a photograph of myself hanging on the wall (along with 199 other Water Rats I must admit).

CHAPTER SIX

[1] *The Magic Circular* (vol. 25), p. 10.

[2] Wass, Verrall. *The Magic Circular* (1954).

[3] *The Sphinx* (vol. 44).

[4] Dornfield, Werner. *The Sphinx*.

[5] Dornfield, "Thirty Years of Magic Thrills," *The Sphinx*.

[6] *Goldston's Magic Annual* (1908/1909), p. 87.

[7] Patent # 15024

[8] Patent # 15025

[9] Latour, Harry. *Abracadabra*.

[10] *The Magic Circular* (October 5th 1954)

[11] *The Magic Circular* (September 8th 1954).

[12] *Magic Annual* (1908/9) pp 88-92)

[13] *The Magic Circular* (1954)

[14] Crayford, Charles. *The Magic Circular*.

[15] *The Magic Circular*. (August 1954).

[16] *Encore* (Feb 24 1956).

CHAPTER SEVEN

[1] Warlock, Peter. *New Pentagram*.

❧ ACKNOWLEDGEMENTS

The research and writing of this book has been exciting, though frustrating at times. However, it could never have been written without the help of so many kind and generous people.

My thanks first to Trudi Couldridge for the start of the initial search, and what a wonderful journey it has been. Also a special acknowledgement to my publisher Gabe Fajuri, designer Kevin McGroarty, and editor Noah Levine. My thanks to Peter Lane for access to his incredible collection and also my extra special thanks to David Ben, Ken Crowe, Will Houstoun, Bill Kalush, Paul Kieve, Eduardo Sanchez of Argentina and, as always, I am grateful for the interest and generosity of John Fisher.

My appreciation also goes to Stan Allen, Alan Astra, Joshua Barr, Maurice Blackman, David Booth, Christopher Brinson, David Budd, Marc Caplan, Mike Caveney, Marshall Colman, George Daily, Anne and John Davenport, L. Davenport Ltd., Professor Eddie Dawes, Trevor Dawson, Timothy Dill-Russell, Paul Draper, David Drummond, The ENO Archive, Mauro Fernandez, Matt Field, John Gaughan, Steve Giles, Brian Glicker, the late Maurice Goldhill, David Gore, Anthony Gross, Richard Hatch, Robin Healey, Ed Hill, David Hibberd, Volker Huber, Chris Izod, Richard Kaufman, Steve Knight, Bob Loomis,

Andy Lansing, Professor David Lewis-Williams, Robin Maddy, Anne Marcus, Jay Marshall, Max Maven, David Meyer, Paul Mogren at Utah Digital Newspapers, Dr. Tim Moore, Robert Olson, the late Patrick Page, Marco Pusterla, Tim Reed, Regina and the late Charles Reynolds, Ricardo Roucau, The Southend Museum, Jim Steinmeyer, Ken Trombly, Jacques Voignier, Neville Wiltshire, and finally Len & Aida Sugarman, Margaret Doser, David March, Lesser Martin, Renee Willman, Jeanette Marchinski and all of the Marchinski family. ✹

❧ NOTE ABOUT THE TYPE

The body of this book is set in the slab-serif font Egyptienne. Another name for slab-serifs is Egyptian, as the first-wave of them were designed in the early 1800s during Napoleon's Egyptian campaign as Egypt-mania swept the western world. Egyptienne was designed in 1956 by Adrian Frutiger.

The sans-serif, Trade Gothic, is a classic of newspapers, advertising, and commercial printing. Trade Gothic was designed in 1948 by Jackson Burke.